RULE THE KITCHEN™

CREATIVE & DELICIOUS RECIPES

FOR YOUR *NINJA® MASTER PREP®* AND *MASTER PREP®* PROFESSIONAL

Cover Design by New Fat Ltd
Published in the United States by

Euro-Pro Operating LLC
Newton, MA
www.ninjakitchen.com

ISBN: 978-0-9838908-0-5

10   11   12   10   9   8   7   6   5
4   3   2   1

TABLE OF CONTENTS

INTRODUCTION • 4

SECRETS TO SUCCESS WITH YOUR *NINJA®*
MASTER PREP® AND *MASTER PREP®* PROFESSIONAL • 5

1 JUICE BLENDS & SMOOTHIES • 7

2 FROZEN DRINK SPECIALTIES • 23

3 COCKTAILS & PARTY DRINKS • 39

4 APPETIZERS, DIPS & SPREADS • 55

5 SOUPS, BISQUE & SAUCES • 73

6 BREADS & BAKERY GOODS • 93

7 ENTRÉES, SALADS & SIDES • 103

8 MARINADES, RUBS & MOPPING SAUCES • 133

9 DESSERTS & SWEET TREATS • 147

10 CONDIMENTS & SPICE BLENDS • 163

11 BABY & TODDLER TREATS • 177

INDEX • 188

INTRODUCTION

The first time the **Ninja® Master Prep®** was seen in action in the **Ninja®** test Kitchen at Euro-Pro, we were all taken aback. We watched with incredulity at the way the **Ninja® Master Prep®** turned solid ice cubes into powdery light 'snow' in a few brief seconds. We knew immediately that we had in our hands, something that was powerful and extremely compact, that we could revolutionise the way millions of people worked in their kitchens, the possibilities were endless.

With **Ninja® Master Prep®** and **Master Prep®** Professionals unique **Ninja®** Blade Technology, it's not only powerful, but versatile. In just 3 split second pulses, the same machine that can obliterate ice cubes, can make a thick and chunky salsa that is evenly chopped.

The secret is in combining the **Ninja®** Blade Technology with incredible power. Quite simply, onions chopped in a conventional machine will be liquefied before the topmost layer can even makes its way to the blades, The **Ninja®** gets the work done in half the time-and with delicate fruits or vegetables, time equals texture.

This is why the **Ninja® Master Prep®** has become indispensable to millions of people worldwide in their every day meals. It's powerful enough to replace their large meat grinders, mixers and other units which take up half their cupboards and quick enough to whip the creamiest chocolate mousse for dessert. It's allowed them to spend less time chopping, dicing, mashing or mixing, and more time with the family or just enjoy, unabated the simple pleasure of cooking – the actual cooking part.

To say the **Ninja® Master Prep®** makes entertaining easier would be a huge understatement. No other machine we know can cater for an entire party, from dips and appetizers to the smoothest, thickest smoothies or cocktails..........with true resort quality consistency.

With the interchangeable **Master Pod™**, you can easily move from chopping in the 16oz chopping bowl to blending in the 48oz pitcher in seconds. The bowl, cup and pitcher are all dishwasher safe, so clean up takes seconds meaning I can get back to guests/family without delay.

The recipes in this book were all specifically written and tested for the **Ninja® Master Prep®** and **Ninja® Master Prep®** Professional; some of these classic recipes have been around since we can remember. Now they are just fresher, and a great deal quicker and easier to prepare.

With the amazing power, performance and versatility of the **Ninja® Master Prep®** and the **Ninja® Master Prep®** Professional and all of these recipes to get you started, grab your **Ninja®** a tray of ice and start to image the possibilities and how you will now '**Rule the Kitchen™**'

SECRETS TO SUCCESS WITH YOUR *NINJA*® *MASTER PREP*® OR YOUR *NINJA*® *MASTER PREP*® PROFESSIONAL

TO GET THE MOST out of your **Ninja® Master Prep®** or your **Ninja® Master Prep®** Professional, just remember these helpful tips:

• Measure your ingredients with accuracy

The results of your recipe will depend on how well you measure the ingredients. Using dry and fluid measuring cups, accurate scales, when needed and measuring with measuring cup (instead of that random spoon out of the draw) will guarantee a success.

• Pulse your way to your desired consistency

The **Ninja® Master Prep®** and the **Ninja® Master Prep®** Professional are meant to be pulsed in quick bursts and will actually work better and faster this way, than simply holding down the button. The stopping and starting literally jolts the food up and down to better mix and chop evenly. When the recipes in this book refer to pulsing in seconds, pulse on and off for the duration of those seconds for the best results.

• Use uniform pieces of food

While the **Ninja® Master Prep®** and **Ninja® Master Prep®** Professional do all of the hard work for you and is quite capable of chopping large pieces of food, mixing similar sized pieces of food at the same time, will give you the most even results. Don't forget, it's so easy to pop off the top that you can pulse uneven pieces in two stages: large pieces first and then the smaller.

• Bigger batches aren't always better

When pulsing chunky or hard food, such as raw vegetables, try not to pack the **Master Prep®** Cup, Bowl or Pitcher to the very top. The **Ninja® Master Prep®** and The **Ninja® Master Prep®** Professional rely on a little bit of room to move the food around to give you the most even and consistent results.

CHAPTER ONE

Juice Blends & Smoothies

BREAKFAST VEGGIE BLEND

SERVES 1

A powerful antioxidant breakfast blend!

240ml vegetable blend juice
30gms fresh carrot, cut into chunks
8 leaves fresh spinach, torn
pinch salt
pinch black pepper

Place all of the ingredients into the bowl. Pulse until smooth. Pour and serve over ice.

TIP

For extra protein power, add up to 10 grams of spinach leaves. You'll have energy for the whole day!

YOU'LL NEED:

✓ 1500ml Pitcher
✓ Blade Assembly
✓ Pitcher Lid

GARDEN IN A GLASS

SERVES 1

Serve icy-cold as an appetizer or chilled as a refreshing beverage. The combined flavours of this blend are very soothing on a hot summer day.

240ml spicy tomato juice
1 teaspoon lemon juice
1 small Roma tomato, cut into quarters
1-inch piece onion, peeled
1-inch piece green bell pepper, seeded
dash Tabasco® sauce
celery stick for garnish

Pour the tomato and lemon juices into the bowl. Add the tomato, onion and green pepper. Add the Tabasco sauce to taste. Pulse until very smooth. Strain, if desired, and pour over ice into a tall glass. Garnish with the celery stick.

✳TIP

Although many people prefer strained juices, unstrained juices contain more fiber and are better for you – give it a try!

YOU'LL NEED:

✓ 1500ml Pitcher
✓ Blade Assembly
✓ Pitcher Lid

VEGGIE IRON POWER PUNCH

SERVES 1

The sweetened tea and apple slices add a hint of sugar to this iron-packed spinach tea.

480ml cold iced tea, sweetened
8 leaves spinach, washed
1 celery stick
½ green apple, cut into pieces

Pour the tea into the bowl and add the spinach, celery and green apple. Pulse until smooth. Strain the drink through a fine sieve and serve in a tall glass over ice.

❋TIP

Start by adding 8 leaves to this recipe and, as you adapt to the flavour, increase the fresh spinach leaves according to your taste. Spinach equals energy!

YOU'LL NEED:

✓ 1500ml Pitcher
✓ Blade Assembly
✓ Pitcher Lid

TRIPLE BERRY TWIST

SERVES 3 TO 4

Substitute any fresh berry and create a new twist of your own.

30gms fresh, ripe raspberries
30gms fresh, ripe blackberries
30gms fresh, ripe strawberries
60ml fat-free, non-dairy vanilla coffee creamer
60ml semi-skimmed or skimmed milk
¼ tablespoon sugar or sugar substitute
190gms ice cubes

Place the fruit in the pitcher and add the creamer, milk and sugar. Add the ice cubes and pulse until completely smooth. Serve right away.

TIP

This recipe is perfect if you are watching your fat and calorie counts!

YOU'LL NEED:

✓ 1500ml Pitcher
✓ Blade Assembly
✓ Pitcher Lid

ORANGE RUSSIAN TEA

SERVES 1

Try this soothing tea whenever you have a sore throat or cold – it's practically medicinal.

240ml water
1 teaspoon instant unsweetened iced tea
240ml orange juice
1 teaspoon whole cloves
½ inch piece whole cinnamon
1 pod cardamom

Place all ingredients into the bowl. Pulse for 20 seconds. Strain the tea through a fine sieve. Microwave or heat in a saucepan on the stove until steaming.

TIP

Make this for a crowd by adjusting the ingredient amounts and add a shot of honey-based Canadian whiskey (such as Yukon Jack™) per serving for a kick of warmth!

YOU'LL NEED:

√ 1500ml Pitcher
√ Blade Assembly
√ Pitcher Lid

STRAWBERRY BANANA SMOOTHIE

SERVES 3

330gms frozen strawberries
2 ripe bananas, peeled
240ml milk
2 tablespoons sugar or 3 packets sugar substitute

Place all the ingredients in the **Master Prep**® Pitcher. Secure the top and pulse for about 45 seconds, until smooth and creamy. Drink should be completely smooth when you no longer hear pieces of frozen strawberry being chopped.

Serve garnished with a fresh strawberry or slice of banana.

TIP

Frozen strawberries sold in the frozen foods section of the grocery store are the easiest and most inexpensive way to make a smoothie, though they are not always the sweetest. Depending on your taste, you may want to add 2 teaspoons or 1 packet of sugar substitute to sweeten things up.

YOU'LL NEED:

✓ **1500ml Pitcher**
✓ **Blade Assembly**
✓ **Pitcher Lid**

RULE THE KITCHE

BERRY MIXED UP SMOOTHIE

SERVES 3

275gms frozen strawberries
65gms frozen blueberries
60gms frozen raspberries
240ml milk
½ teaspoon vanilla extract
2 tablespoons sugar or 3 packets sugar substitute

Place all ingredients in the **Master Prep®** Pitcher. Secure the top and pulse for about 45 seconds, until smooth and creamy. Drink should be completely smooth when you no longer hear pieces of frozen berries being chopped.

Serve garnished with whipped cream, fresh berries, or both!

TIP

For a great breakfast smoothie, 330ml of fresh vanilla yogurt can be substituted for the milk, vanilla extract and sugar in this recipe. Or try a blueberry or raspberry yogurt for even more berry goodness!

YOU'LL NEED:

✓ **1500ml Pitcher**
✓ **Blade Assembly**
✓ **Pitcher Lid**

HEALTHY FRUIT AND VEGETABLE SMOOTHIE

SERVES 4

240ml pineapple juice
1 small carrot
120gms cherry tomatoes
½ apple, unpeeled and cut in half again
1 kiwi, peeled
2 wedges watermelon, 2 inches thick each
1 wedge cantaloupe, 2 inches thick
6 strawberries
20 gms fresh spinach
1 slice ginger, ¼ inch thick
½ celery stick
2 tablespoons sugar or 3 packets sugar substitute
6 ice cubes

Place all the ingredients in the **Master Prep**® Pitcher, ice cubes on top. Secure the top and pulse for about 60 seconds, until the entire drink is liquefied. Drink should be completely liquefied when you no longer hear pieces of ice being chopped.

Serve garnished with fresh fruit.

 TIP

The taste of this healthy smoothie is delicious when all of the ingredients are well combined, so be sure that you pulse it long enough to completely liquefy.

YOU'LL NEED:

✓ **1500ml Pitcher**
✓ **Blade Assembly**
✓ **Pitcher Lid**

TROPICAL PARADISE BLEND

SERVES 2

220gms frozen mango
1 kiwi, peeled and quartered
120ml pineapple juice
120ml milk
1½ tablespoons sugar or 2 packets sugar substitute

Place all ingredients in the **Master Prep®** Pitcher. Secure the top and pulse for about 45 seconds, until smooth and creamy. Drink should be completely smooth when you no longer hear pieces of frozen mango being chopped.

Serve garnished with a slice of fresh kiwi.

TIP

Try adding a scoop of low-fat vanilla ice cream or frozen yogurt to any smoothie for an even creamier drink. Replace the milk with coconut milk for something even more tropical!

YOU'LL NEED:

✓ **1500ml Pitcher**
✓ **Blade Assembly**
✓ **Pitcher Lid**

PROTEIN PACKED MOCHA SMOOTHIE

SERVES 2

225 gms tofu, drained and cubed
240ml vanilla yoghurt
2 tablespoons chocolate syrup
1½ teaspoons instant coffee
1½ tablespoons sugar or 2 packets sugar substitute
8 ice cubes

Place all the ingredients in the **Master Prep**® Pitcher, ice cubes on top. Secure the Pitcher's top and pulse for about 45 seconds, until smooth and creamy. Drink should be completely smooth when you no longer hear pieces of ice being chopped.

Serve topped with a drizzle of chocolate syrup.

TIP

Add a frozen banana for a thicker, creamer, Banana Mocha Smoothie. 2 scoops of a chocolate flavoured protein powder and 4 extra ice cubes can be substituted in a place of the tofu and chocolate syrup.

YOU'LL NEED:

✓ 1500ml Pitcher
✓ Blade Assembly
✓ Pitcher Lid

RULE THE KITCHEN

MANDARIN ORANGE SMOOTHIE

SERVES 4

2 cans (280gms each) mandarin orange segments,
drained
125gms ice
240ml vanilla non-fat yoghurt
120ml orange juice
120ml carrot juice

❋ TIP

Whenever I am buying canned fruit, I always look for the cans that pack the fruit in 100% juice, not heavy or light syrup. All of the extra sugar in the syrup is not only bad for you, but really takes away from the natural flavour of the fruit.

Place drained oranges into freezer for at least 2 hours, or until frozen solid.

Place frozen oranges and ice in the **Master Prep®** Pitcher. Secure the Pitcher's top and pulse for 7-10 short pulses, or until snow.

Add vanilla yogurt, orange juice, and carrot juice, re-secure the Pitcher's top and pulse for 5-7 long pulses, or until smooth and creamy.

Serve garnished with a wedge of fresh orange.

YOU'LL NEED:

✓ **1500ml Pitcher**
✓ **Blade Assembly**
✓ **Pitcher Lid**

GREEN APPLE GOODNESS SMOOTHIE

SERVES 2

2 green apples, peeled and cored
1 kiwi, peeled
240ml white grape juice
1½ tablespoons sugar or 2 packets sugar substitute
6 ice cubes

Place all the ingredients in the **Master Prep**® Pitcher, ice cubes on top. Secure the Pitcher's top and pulse for about 60 seconds, until smooth. Drink should be completely smooth when you no longer hear pieces of ice being chopped.

Serve immediately, topped with a slice of unpeeled, green apple.

YOU'LL NEED:

✓ 1500ml Pitcher
✓ Blade Assembly
✓ Pitcher Lid

RULE THE KITCHEN

HONEY SWEET PEACH SMOOTHIE

SERVES 2

250 gms frozen peach slices
240ml peach yoghurt
120ml milk
1 tablespoon honey

Place frozen peach slices in the **Master Prep®** Pitcher and then cover with remaining ingredients. Secure the Pitcher's top and pulse for about 45 seconds, until smooth and creamy. Drink should be completely smooth when you no longer hear pieces of frozen peach being chopped.

Serve garnished with a light sprinkling of cinnamon, if desired.

YOU'LL NEED:

√ 1500ml Pitcher
√ Blade Assembly
√ Pitcher Lid

CRANRAZZ SMOOTHIE

SERVES 2

120gms frozen raspberries
360ml vanilla frozen yoghurt
360ml cranberry juice cocktail

Place all the ingredients in the **Master Prep®** Pitcher. Secure the top and pulse for about 45 seconds, until smooth and creamy. Drink should be completely smooth when you no longer hear pieces of frozen raspberries being chopped.

Serve garnished with a fresh raspberry.

TIP

Try substituting orange sherbet for the frozen yogurt in this recipe for a citrus twist on this great smoothie! For a fresher orange taste, skip the sherbet in lieu of a teaspoon of orange zest and save the meat of the orange for a garnish.

YOU'LL NEED:

✓ **1500ml Pitcher**
✓ **Blade Assembly**
✓ **Pitcher Lid**

ORANGE CREAM
P. 33

CHAPTER TWO
Frozen Drink Specialties

FRESH WATERMELON SLUSH

SERVES 3

600gms watermelon, seeded and cubed
240ml lemon lime soda

✳TIP

Depending on how ripe the watermelon is, you may want to add a dash of sugar or sugar substitute to sweeten things up. Add a kiwi and replace the lemon lime soda with white grape juice for a different drink altogether!

Place cubed watermelon into freezer for at least 2 hours, until frozen solid.

Place frozen watermelon cubes in the **Master Prep**® Pitcher and then add lemon lime soda over top. Secure the top and pulse for 10-20 seconds, until smooth and creamy.

Serve garnished with a wedge of fresh watermelon or lime.

YOU'LL NEED:

✓ **1500ml Pitcher**
✓ **Blade Assembly**
✓ **Pitcher Lid**

MOCHA CAPPUCCINO

SERVES 2

240ml espresso
360ml milk
6 teaspoons sugar or 3 packets sugar substitute
2 tablespoons chocolate syrup
whipped cream, for garnish

Fill one half of a 16 cube ice cube tray with espresso and the other half with 240ml milk. Freeze for at least 3 hours, or until frozen solid.

Place espresso and milk cubes in the **Master Prep®** Pitcher and then add sugar, chocolate syrup and the remaining 120ml of milk over top. Secure the top and pulse for 10-20 seconds, until smooth and creamy.

Serve with whipped cream.

YOU'LL NEED:

✓ 1500ml Pitcher
✓ Blade Assembly
✓ Pitcher Lid

RULE THE KITCHE

APPLE CARROT BLAST

SERVES 2

240ml carrot juice
360ml apple juice
1 teaspoon lemon juice

Fill one half of a 16 cube ice cube tray with carrot juice and the other half with 240ml of the apple juice. Freeze for at least 3 hours, or until frozen solid.

Place carrot and apple juice cubes in the *Master Prep®* Pitcher and then the lemon juice and 120ml of apple juice over top. Secure the Pitcher's top and pulse for 10-20 seconds, until smooth and creamy. Serve immediately.

YOU'LL NEED:

✓ 1500ml Pitcher
✓ Blade Assembly
✓ Pitcher Lid

FROZEN LEMONADE

SERVES 2

600ml lemonade

1 teaspoon lemon zest

2 teaspoons sugar or 1 packet sugar substitute

Fill one 16 cube ice cube tray with lemonade. Freeze for at least 3 hours, or until frozen solid.

Place lemonade cubes in the **Master Prep**® Pitcher and then add lemon zest and the remaining 120ml of lemonade over top. Secure the Pitcher's top and pulse for 10-20 seconds, until smooth and creamy. Serve garnished with a lemon wedge.

YOU'LL NEED:

✓ 1500ml Pitcher

✓ Blade Assembly

✓ Pitcher Lid

PINEAPPLE BREEZE

SERVES 2

480ml pineapple juice
120ml coconut milk

Fill one 16 cube ice cube tray with pineapple juice. Freeze for at least 3 hours, or until frozen solid.

Place pineapple juice cubes in the **Master Prep®** Pitcher and then add coconut milk over top. Secure the Pitcher's top and pulse for 10-20 seconds, until smooth and creamy. Serve garnished with toasted coconut or a wedge of fresh pineapple.

YOU'LL NEED:

✓ 1500ml Pitcher
✓ Blade Assembly
✓ Pitcher Lid

CRANBERRY TWIST

SERVES 2

480ml cranberry juice cocktail
120ml white grape juice
Juice of 1 lime
2 teaspoons sugar or 1 packet sugar substitute

Fill one 16 cube ice cube tray with cranberry juice. Freeze for at least 3 hours, or until frozen solid.

Place cranberry juice cubes in the **Master Prep®** Pitcher and then add white grape juice, lime juice and sugar over top. Secure the Pitcher's top and pulse for 10-20 seconds, until smooth and creamy.

Serve garnished with a wedge of lime.

TIP

A lime yields about 2 tablespoons of lime juice, if you would rather substitute bottled juice for this recipe. If using 100% cranberry juice instead of cranberry juice cocktail with sugar added, you may want to double or triple the sugar to offset the tartness.

YOU'LL NEED:

✓ 1500ml Pitcher
✓ Blade Assembly
✓ Pitcher Lid

"WHITE" MANGO ICE

SERVES 2

480ml mango nectar or juice
120ml white grape juice

Fill one 16 cube ice cube tray with mango nectar. Freeze for at least 3 hours, or until frozen solid.

Place mango cubes in the **Master Prep**® Pitcher and then white grape juice over top. Secure the Pitcher's top and pulse for 10-20 seconds, until smooth and creamy.

Serve garnished with fresh mango or a pineapple ring.

✳TIP

Mango nectar is usually found in cartons in the Spanish food aisle. If you are having trouble locating it, many companies sell some kind of mango juice cocktail in the regular juice aisle and even in the refrigerated section near the orange juice.

YOU'LL NEED:

✓ 1500ml Pitcher
✓ Blade Assembly
✓ Pitcher Lid

NINJA® SNOW CONES

SERVES 2

Ice
flavoured syrup or powdered drink mix

☀TIP

Snow cone syrups may not be sold in your local grocery store, but are almost always sold in Super discount stores. The variety of flavours is usually not as large as just making your own out of powdered drink mix.

To make snow in the **Ninja® Master Prep**®, fill the **Master Prep**® Pitcher with ice, no more than two-thirds of the way up. There is no need to add any additional liquid.

Secure the Pitcher's top and pulse in short bursts for 10-20 seconds, or until ice is completely pulverized into a fine powder. Use an ice cream scoop to scoop into a glass or paper cone cup.

Top with store bought snow cone syrups. To make your own syrups: follow the directions on any packet of powdered drink mix using the correct ratio of mix and sugar, but only ⅓ of the water. Heat in a sauce pan over medium-low heat until it simmers and sugar has dissolved. Refrigerate the resulting syrup until cooled.

YOU'LL NEED:

✓ 1500ml Pitcher
✓ Blade Assembly
✓ Pitcher Lid

VANILLA COFFEE ICE

SERVES 2

480ml coffee

120ml milk

2 tablespoons sugar or 3 packets sugar substitute

1 teaspoon vanilla extract

whipped cream, for garnish

✳TIP

I prefer natural vanilla extract over the imitation vanilla extract for the best flavour. You can also skip the vanilla extract and sugar in lieu of 2 tablespoons vanilla coffee syrup, usually sold in clear plastic bottles in the coffee aisle.

Fill a 16 cube ice cube tray with coffee. Freeze for at least 3 hours, or until frozen solid.

Place coffee cubes in the **Master Prep®** Pitcher and then add milk, sugar and vanilla extract over top. Secure the Pitcher's top and pulse for 10-20 seconds, until smooth and creamy.

Serve garnished with whipped cream.

YOU'LL NEED:

✓ 1500ml Pitcher

✓ Blade Assembly

✓ Pitcher Lid

ORANGE AND CREAM

SERVES 2

240ml vanilla yoghurt
360ml orange soda
whipped cream, for garnish

Fill one half of a 16 cube ice cube tray with vanilla yogurt and the other half with 240ml of orange soda. Freeze for at least 3 hours, or until frozen solid.

Place yogurt and orange soda cubes in the **Master Prep®** Pitcher and then add the remaining 120ml of orange soda over top. Secure the Pitcher's top and pulse for 10-20 seconds, until smooth and creamy.

Add sugar to taste, if desired. Serve garnished with whipped cream.

✳ TIP

In a pinch, milk and 1 teaspoon of vanilla extract can be substituted for the vanilla yogurt in this recipe. Orange juice can be substituted for the orange soda.

YOU'LL NEED:

✓ 1500ml Pitcher
✓ Blade Assembly
✓ Pitcher Lid

KEY LIME PIE ICE

SERVES 2

360ml milk

240ml limeade

½ teaspoon vanilla extract

4 teaspoons sugar or 2 packets sugar substitute

Fill one half of a 16 cube ice cube tray with 240ml milk and the other half of the tray with limeade. Freeze for at least 3 hours, or until frozen solid.

Place milk and limeade cubes in the **Master Prep®** Pitcher and then add the vanilla extract, sugar and the remaining 120ml of milk over top. Secure the Pitcher's top and pulse for 10-20 seconds, until smooth and creamy.

Serve garnished with a lime wedge.

✳TIP

If the limeade you are using is sweet, but not very tart, add an additional tablespoon of lime or key lime juice to give the drink a little kick.

YOU'LL NEED:

✓ 1500ml Pitcher

✓ Blade Assembly

✓ Pitcher Lid

CHOCOLATE RASPBERRY RUMBLE

SERVES 2

480ml milk
1½ tablespoons chocolate syrup
4 teaspoons sugar or 2 packets sugar substitute
2 tablespoons raspberry preserve

✳TIP

This drink, or any of my frozen speciality drinks in this book, can be made lighter by substituting soy milk for the milk. Fat free milk also works well, but I actually find the soy milk to be thicker and more decadent.

Fill a 16 cube ice cube tray with milk. Freeze for at least 3 hours, or until frozen solid.

Place milk cubes in the **Master Prep**® Pitcher and then chocolate syrup, sugar, raspberry preserves and the other 120ml of milk over top. Secure the Pitcher's top and pulse for 10-20 seconds, until smooth and creamy.

Serve immediately garnished with fresh raspberries or shaved chocolate or both!

YOU'LL NEED:

✓ 1500ml Pitcher
✓ Blade Assembly
✓ Pitcher Lid

COOKIES AND CREAM MILKSHAKE

SERVES 2

480ml vanilla ice cream (2 large scoops)
360ml milk
½ teaspoon vanilla extract
2 ice cubes
6 cream filled chocolate sandwich cookies

✳TIP

I'm pretty sure you know which brand of cookie I'm referring to here, but just in case, let me tell you a story-o about a boy name Or… never mind.

Place ice cream, milk, vanilla extract and ice cubes in the **Master Prep®** Pitcher, ice cubes on top. Secure the Pitcher's top and pulse for about 30 seconds, until ice cubes are almost entirely broken up.

Add in chocolate sandwich cookies and re-secure the Pitcher's top. Pulse for 15 more seconds until milkshake is speckled with cookie bits, but cookies are not entirely liquefied.

Serve topped with whipped cream and a whole chocolate sandwich cookie.

YOU'LL NEED:

✓ 1500ml Pitcher
✓ Blade Assembly
✓ Pitcher Lid

PEACHES AND CREAM MILKSHAKE

SERVES 2

480ml vanilla ice cream (2 large scoops)
360ml milk
1 teaspoon vanilla extract
2 teaspoons sugar or 1 packet sugar substitute
2 ice cubes
1 peach, pitted and sliced

✳ TIP

This recipe works well with nectarines or apricots too. You may even want to try it with more tropical fruits like pineapple, papaya or mango. Simply substitute 125gms of any fruit in place of the peach.

Place ice cream, milk, vanilla extract, sugar and ice cubes in the **Master Prep**® Pitcher, ice cubes on top. Secure the Pitcher's top and pulse for about 30 seconds, until ice cubes are almost entirely broken up.

Add in peach slices and re-secure the Pitcher's top. Pulse for 15 more seconds until peach slices are chopped into small pieces, but not entirely liquefied.

Serve topped with whipped cream and a fresh peach wedge.

YOU'LL NEED:

✓ 1500ml Pitcher
✓ Blade Assembly
✓ Pitcher Lid

CHAPTER THREE

Cocktails & Party Drinks

THE BEST FROZEN MARGARITA

SERVES 4

625gms ice
1 can (180ml) frozen limeade concentrate
180ml tequila
60ml triple sec
Margarita salt, optional

Fill the **Master Prep®** Pitcher with ice half way between 1000ml and 1250ml.

Cover ice with limeade concentrate, tequila and triple sec. Secure the Pitcher's top and pulse for 10-20 seconds, until smooth and creamy.

Serve garnished with Margarita salt and a lime wedge.

✳ TIP

To make Strawberry Margaritas: halve the limeade concentrate and substitute 330gms of frozen strawberries for 375gms of the ice.

YOU'LL NEED:

✓ 1500ml Pitcher
✓ Blade Assembly
✓ Pitcher Lid

40

CREAMY PINA COLADA

SERVES 4

625gms ice
240ml light rum
180ml coconut cream
150gms canned crushed pineapple with juice

Fill the **Master Prep**® Pitcher with ice half way between 1000ml and 1250ml.

Cover ice with rum, coconut cream and pineapple. Secure the Pitcher's top and pulse for 10-20 seconds, until smooth and creamy.

Serve garnished with fresh pineapple or maraschino cherries.

✳ TIP

Coconut cream is usually sold near the thinner coconut milk, but coconut milk will work in a pinch. For a smoother consistency, substitute pineapple juice for the crushed pineapple.

YOU'LL NEED:

✓ 1500ml Pitcher
✓ Blade Assembly
✓ Pitcher Lid

STRAWBERRY DAIQUIRI

SERVES 4

250gms ice
330gms frozen strawberries
240ml light rum
120ml lime juice
70gms sugar

Place ice, frozen strawberries, rum, lime juice and sugar in the **Master Prep**® Pitcher. Secure the Pitcher's top and pulse for 10-20 seconds, until smooth and creamy.

Serve garnished with a fresh strawberry or a wedge of lime.

YOU'LL NEED:

✓ 1500ml Pitcher
✓ Blade Assembly
✓ Pitcher Lid

PEACH DAIQUIRI

SERVES 4

250gms ice
375 gms frozen peaches
120ml white rum
120ml peach schnapps
60ml lime juice
50gms sugar

Place ice, frozen peaches, white rum, peach schnapps, lime juice and sugar in the **Master Prep®** Pitcher. Secure the Pitcher's top and pulse for 10-20 seconds, until smooth and creamy.

Serve garnished with a sprig of mint or fresh peach wedge.

YOU'LL NEED:

✓ 1500ml Pitcher
✓ Blade Assembly
✓ Pitcher Lid

MUDSLIDE

SERVES 4

625gms ice
60ml vodka
90ml coffee liqueur
90ml Irish cream liqueur
2 tablespoons chocolate syrup
whipped cream

✳ TIP

Coffee liqueur may be a little pricey, especially with two other spirits to purchase. A double shot of chilled espresso may be substituted as long as you double the amount of Irish Cream liqueur.

Fill the **Master Prep®** Pitcher with ice half way between 1000ml and 1250ml.

Cover ice with vodka, coffee liqueur, Irish cream liqueur and chocolate syrup. Secure the Pitcher's top and pulse for 10-20 seconds, until smooth and creamy.

Serve topped with whipped cream and a drizzle of chocolate syrup.

YOU'LL NEED:

✓ 1500ml Pitcher
✓ Blade Assembly
✓ Pitcher Lid

STRAWBERRY MANGO COLADA

SERVES 4

Strawberry Colada
125gms ice
120ml light rum
60ml coconut cream
220gms frozen strawberries

Mango Colada
125gms ice
120ml light rum
120ml coconut cream
220gms frozen mango chunks

✳ TIP

To toast grated coconut: preheat the oven to 350 degrees Fahrenheit, 180 degrees Celsius or Gas Mark 4 and spread coconut on a sheet pan in a thin layer. Bake 6-8 minutes, shaking sheet pan halfway through to stir around.

Place ice, rum, coconut cream and frozen strawberries in the **Master Prep®** Pitcher. Secure the Pitcher's top and pulse for 10-20 seconds, until smooth and creamy. Transfer mixture to a separate Pitcher or use a second **Master Prep®** Pitcher for the second half of the drink.

Place ice, rum, coconut cream and frozen mango in an empty **Master Prep®** Pitcher. Secure the Pitcher's top and pulse for 10-20 seconds, until smooth and creamy.

Layer the Strawberry and Mango Coladas in 1-2 inch layers, tapping the glass to settle before adding each layer on top of the other.

Serve garnished with toasted coconut or fresh fruit.

YOU'LL NEED:

✓ 1500ml Pitcher
✓ Blade Assembly
✓ Pitcher Lid

FROZEN BLUE BAYOU

MAKES 2 TO 3 SERVINGS

This cool refresher is made with Blue Curacao, an orange flavoured liqueur that originated in the Caribbean. It is now produced mainly in France and is available in many colours.

250gms ice cubes, crushed
90ml good quality vodka
60ml Blue Curacao
240ml lemonade
2 to 3 frozen lime wedges for garnish

Place the ice into the pitcher and add the remaining ingredients, except the lime wedges. Pulse until smooth. Pour into tall chilled glasses and garnish with lime wedges.

TIP

Invest in a bottle of Blue Curacao, which is reasonably priced, for a splash of colour and flavour at your next party. The vivid blue colour alone invites a happy response from each guest!

YOU'LL NEED:

✓ 1500ml Pitcher
✓ Blade Assembly
✓ Pitcher Lid

PINEAPPLE MANGO MOJITO

MAKES 2 SERVINGS

It's hard to make a classic Mojito more tropical than it already is, but this really does the trick.

75gms fresh pineapple chunks
55gms fresh mango chunks
30ml fresh lime juice
1 tablespoons icing sugar
5 to 6 mint leaves
90ml light rum
240ml sparkling water
250gms ice cubes

Garnish
15gm icing sugar
2 lime slices
2 sprigs of mint

Place the pineapple, mango, lime juice, sugar and mint into the pitcher and pulse until smooth. Add the rum and 240ml sparkling water and pulse until just blended.

Sprinkle the sugar onto a shallow saucer. Moisten the rim of each glass with lime and dip the rim of the glass into the sugar. Add the ice to the prepared glasses and fill each with the Pineapple Mango Mojito. Garnish with lime slices and a sprig of mint.

YOU'LL NEED:

✓ 1500ml Pitcher
✓ Blade Assembly
✓ Pitcher Lid

FROZEN CUBAN MOJITO

MAKES 1 SERVINGS

This minty refresher will have you dreaming of Old Havana.

30ml simple syrup (recipe follows)
30ml fresh lime juice
5 fresh mint leaves
140ml light rum
190gms ice cubes
1 mint sprigs for garnish

Simple Syrup
60ml water
25gms sugar

Place the simple syrup, lime juice and mint leaves into the pitcher and pulse until combined. Add the rum and crushed ice and pulse until smooth. Pour into lowball glasses and garnish with mint sprigs.

Simple Syrup: Combine water and sugar in a small sauce pan and bring to a boil. Simmer, while stirring, over low heat until the sugar dissolves. Cool to room temperature. Store in the refrigerator in a glass bottle.

YOU'LL NEED:

✓ 1500ml Pitcher
✓ Blade Assembly
✓ Pitcher Lid

ITALIAN BELLINI

MAKES 2 SERVINGS

The Bellini was invented in 1948 at Harry's Bar in Venice, Italy, a known hang-out of writer Ernest Hemingway.

3 medium white peaches, pitted and peeled
½ bottle Italian sparkling wine, chilled
(recommend Prosecco)
2 splashes Crème de framboise

Place the peaches into the pitcher and pulse until uniformly smooth. Spoon the pureed peaches into four champagne flutes. Top the peach puree with a splash of Crème de framboise and fill with the Italian sparkling wine.

✳ TIP

For a touch of delight, serve these Bellinis with rich shortbread cookies.

YOU'LL NEED:

✓ 1500ml Pitcher
✓ Blade Assembly
✓ Pitcher Lid

BUSHWACKER

MAKES 2 SERVINGS

Beware the Bushwacker! This cocktail really packs a punch, hence the name.

30ml dark rum
30ml Kahlua
30ml dark crème de cacao
30ml coconut liqueur
600ml double cream
125gms crushed ice cubes

Garnish
Whipped cream
Ground nutmeg

Place all ingredients, except the whipped cream and nutmeg, into the pitcher and pulse until smooth. Pour into tall glasses and garnish with whipped cream and a sprinkle of nutmeg.

✳ TIP

Change this up by substituting cream of coconut for the coconut liqueur, amaretto for the Kahlua, or try using equal portions of dark and light rum. Every substitution creates an entirely new drink, worthy of tasting and testing among friends!

YOU'LL NEED:

✓ 1500ml Pitcher
✓ Blade Assembly
✓ Pitcher Lid

SOUTH PACIFIC SLUSH

MAKES 1 SERVINGS

You will be able to hear the ocean breeze blowing through the palm trees as you sip this delicious island sensation.

125gms crushed ice cubes
60ml dark rum
60ml orange juice
30ml coconut milk
½ banana, peeled
1 tablespoons lime juice

Garnish
4 pineapple chunks
2 orange wedges, halved
1 thin wooden skewers
1 splashes grenadine

Place the ice cubes into the pitcher, add the remaining ingredients, except the garnish, and pulse until slushy-smooth.

Thread the pineapple chunks and orange wedges alternately onto skewers. Pour the drinks into tall, chilled glasses and garnish with the fruit skewers and a splash of grenadine.

YOU'LL NEED:

✓ 1500ml Pitcher
✓ Blade Assembly
✓ Pitcher Lid

SEA BREEZE SOOTHER

MAKES 2 SERVINGS

To create a Hawaiian Sea Breeze, replace the grapefruit juice with pineapple juice.

120ml good quality vodka
180ml cranberry juice
180ml grapefruit juice
250gms crushed ice cubes
2 lime slices for garnish

Pour the vodka, cranberry juice and grapefruit juice into the pitcher and pulse until mixed and frothy.

Place the ice in chilled glasses, fill each with the drink and garnish with the lime slices.

TIP

This is the perfect cocktail for those who prefer tart and tangy over sweet. Serve with southwestern foods or whole grain crackers and a cheese spread. The full flavour of this drink can accompany hearty foods without becoming overwhelmed.

YOU'LL NEED:

✓ 1500ml Pitcher
✓ Blade Assembly
✓ Pitcher Lid

RULE THE KITCH

ROASTED
TOMATO & OLIVE
BRUSCHETTA
P. 71

CHAPTER FOUR

Appetizers, Dips & Spreads

HERBED CHEESE DIP

SERVES 6

20gms Parmesan cheese
2 cloves garlic, peeled
1 teaspoon lemon juice
1 tablespoon fresh parsley
1 tablespoon fresh chives
1 tablespoon fresh basil
½ teaspoon onion powder
240gms cream cheese
salt and pepper to taste

✳TIP

Just about any fresh herbs work well in this recipe. Try oregano or thyme in place of the basil or even 2 teaspoons of dried Italian seasoning if you're in a pinch. Low-fat or even fat-free cream cheese works great to for the best low-fat dip around!

Place Parmesan cheese, garlic, lemon juice, parsley, chives, basil and onion powder in the **Master Prep**® Processing Bowl. Secure top and pulse in quick bursts until Parmesan cheese is almost grated. If starting with grated Parmesan cheese, pulse until herbs are finely chopped.

Remove top and use a spoon to push mixture down, away from the walls of the Bowl.

Add cream cheese, re-secure top and pulse in quick bursts for 15 seconds, until cheese and herbs are well combined.

Salt and pepper to taste and serve immediately or cover and refrigerate for up to 4 days.

YOU'LL NEED:

✓ 1200ml Bowl
✓ Blade Assembly
✓ Bowl Lid

MICROWAVE SPINACH AND ARTICHOKE DIP

SERVES 8

240ml double cream
240gms reduced-fat cream cheese
120gms Parmesan cheese
2 cloves garlic, peeled
½ teaspoon salt
¼ teaspoon ground black pepper
150 gms canned artichoke hearts, drained
300gms frozen spinach, thawed

✳**TIP**

Make your own flour tortilla chips for dipping by frying fresh tortillas in a lightly buttered pan until golden brown. While traditionally served hot, this dip works just fine cold as well… simply skip the microwave.

Place all ingredients in the **Master Prep®** Processing Bowl, artichokes and spinach on top. Secure the top and pulse 5-7 times until combined, but chunky.

Carefully remove blades from the **Master Prep®** Processing Bowl and microwave dip for 2 minutes, stirring halfway through.

Serve as a hot dip for tortilla chips, garnished with a whole artichoke heart and grated or grated Parmesan cheese.

YOU'LL NEED:

✓ 1200ml Bowl
✓ Blade Assembly
✓ Bowl Lid

RULE THE KITCHEN

THICK AND CHUNKY GUACAMOLE

SERVES 6

2 ripe hass avocados
½ of 1 onion, cut in half
1 jalapeño pepper, ends trimmed and seeds scraped out
8 cherry tomatoes
juice of 1 lime
60 ml sour cream
5gms fresh coriander
salt and pepper to taste

✳TIP

The lime juice in this recipe will keep the avocado from turning brown. To keep the guacamole as green as it can be, you may want to drizzle some of the lime juice straight onto the avocado immediately after cutting.

Cut avocados in half by inserting a knife down the centre until it touches the pit, then carefully rotating the avocado until it is sliced through on all sides. Separate the two halves, remove the pit and discard. Use a spoon to scoop the meat out, tracing along the inner skin of the avocado.

Place all the ingredients in the **Master Prep®** Processing Bowl, onion first and coriander last. Top with the peeled avocado. Secure the Bowl's top and pulse 2-3 times for a chunky guacamole. Pulse a few times more for a smoother guacamole dip.

Salt and pepper to taste and serve with tortilla chips or alongside fajitas and burritos.

YOU'LL NEED:

✓ 1200ml Bowl
✓ Blade Assembly
✓ Bowl Lid

MEXICAN CHEESE DIP

SERVES 6

240gms sour cream
120gms reduced-fat cream cheese
4 slices processed American Cheese
¼ of 1 onion
1 jalapeño pepper, ends trimmed and seeds scraped out
1 tomato, top trimmed off and quartered
½ teaspoon cumin
½ teaspoon salt

✳TIP

I prefer white American cheese in this recipe, but a 1 inch slice of a bricked processed cheese like Velveeta melts very well.

Place all the ingredients in the **Master Prep®** Processing Bowl. Secure the top and pulse 5-7 times, or until combined, but chunky.

Carefully remove blades from the **Master Prep®** Processing Bowl and microwave dip for 2 minutes, stirring halfway through.

Serve as a hot dip for tortilla chips.

YOU'LL NEED:

✓ 1200ml Bowl
✓ Blade Assembly
✓ Bowl Lid

RULE THE KITCHE

TUSCAN WHITE BEAN DIP

SERVES 6

1 can (420gm) cannellini beans, drained
60ml olive oil
2 tablespoons lemon juice
2 cloves garlic, peeled
2 teaspoons fresh oregano leaves
1 teaspoon salt
½ teaspoon ground black pepper

Place all the ingredients in the **Master Prep®** Processing Bowl. Secure the top and pulse for 10 long pulses, or until smooth and creamy.

Serve with toasted or grilled pitta bread, pitta chips, crusty baked toast rounds or rustic crackers.

YOU'LL NEED:

✓ 1200ml Bowl
✓ Blade Assembly
✓ Bowl Lid

CLASSIC HUMMUS

SERVES 6

1 can (420gm) garbanzo beans, drained
1½ tablespoons tahini sesame paste
2 cloves garlic, peeled
3 tablespoons lemon juice
½ teaspoon ground cumin
¼ teaspoon paprika
salt to taste

Place all ingredients in the **Master Prep**® Processing Bowl. Secure the top and pulse in 10 long pulses, or until smooth and creamy.

Serve with warmed, toasted or grilled pitta bread, pitta chips, flour tortilla chips, crusty baked toast rounds or rustic crackers.

YOU'LL NEED:

✓ 1200ml Bowl
✓ Blade Assembly
✓ Bowl Lid

RULE THE KITCHE

ROASTED PEPPER CHEESE DIP

SERVES 8

1 jar (210gm) roasted red peppers, drained
¼ of 1 red onion
120ml plain yoghurt
120ml mayonnaise
240gms reduced-fat cream cheese
120gms Cheddar cheese
2 cloves garlic, peeled
1 tablespoon Dijon mustard
½ teaspoon paprika

Place all ingredients in the **Master Prep®** Processing Bowl. Secure the top and pulse 8-10 times until well combined.

Carefully remove blades from the **Master Prep®** Processing Bowl and microwave dip for 2 minutes, stirring halfway through.

Serve as a hot dip for tortilla chips, grilled pittas, pitta chips, toasted bread rounds or vegetables.

TIP

Try caramelizing the onions in a sauté pan before preparing the dip for even more flavour. Add a few drops of smoked jalapeno pepper hot sauce for a little more spice.

YOU'LL NEED:

✓ 1200ml Bowl
✓ Blade Assembly
✓ Bowl Lid

CHUNKY OLIVE SPREAD

SERVES 8

3 cloves garlic, peeled
150gms black olives, pitted
150gms green olives, pitted
150gms kalamata olives, pitted
80ml olive oil
2 teaspoons lemon zest
¼ teaspoon ground black pepper
2 tablespoons fresh parsley

Place all ingredients in the **Master Prep**® Processing Bowl, garlic at the bottom and parsley on top. Secure the top and pulse 5-7 times, until chunky, but well combined.

Serve with crackers or on toasted bread rounds.

✳TIP

Drain and add a small jar (120gms) of roasted red peppers to bring a little more colour (and flavour!) into your next party. Sun-dried tomatoes are yet another great addition.

YOU'LL NEED:

✓ 1200ml Bowl
✓ Blade Assembly
✓ Bowl Lid

RULE THE KITCH

FRESH TOMATO SALSA

SERVES 4

½ of 1 onion, cut in half
1 jalapeño pepper, ends trimmed and seeds scraped out
2 tomatoes, tops trimmed off and quartered
juice of 1 lime
10gms fresh coriander
salt and pepper to taste

Place all ingredients in the **Master Prep®** Processing Bowl, onion first and coriander last. Secure the top and pulse 2-3 times for a chunky salsa. Pulse a few times more for a smoother salsa or taco sauce.

Salt and pepper to taste and serve with tortilla chips, tacos or burritos.

❋TIP

To make a quick and easy tortilla dip, add 1 batch of Fresh Tomato Salsa to 1 tub of sour cream (480ml). Stir until well combined and dip in!

YOU'LL NEED:

✓ 1200ml Bowl
✓ Blade Assembly
✓ Bowl Lid

SALSA VERDE

SERVES 8 - 10

1 small onion, peeled and quartered
3 cloves garlic, peeled
10gms fresh coriander
1 jalapeño, end trimmed and seeds removed
1 tablespoon vegetable oil
1 teaspoon salt
1 can (840gm) tomatillos, drained

Place onion, garlic, coriander, jalapeño, vegetable oil and salt in the **Master Prep**® Processing Bowl. Secure top and pulse in 5 quick pulses, until vegetables begin to break up.

Remove top and use a spoon to push mixture down, away from the walls of the Pitcher.

Add tomatillos, re-secure top and pulse in 5-7 long pulses, until salsa is nearly smooth. Serve at room temperature or refrigerate and serve chilled.

✳ TIP

This recipe is pretty mild, so if you like it hot simply leave the jalapeño's seeds (where most of its heat is found) intact. Add a second jalapeño to go even hotter.

YOU'LL NEED:

✓ 1200ml Bowl
✓ Blade Assembly
✓ Bowl Lid

SWEET AND SPICY PINEAPPLE SALSA

SERVES 6

¼ of 1 red onion, peeled
300gms fresh pineapple chunks
½ red bell pepper, top trimmed off
1 jalapeño pepper, ends trimmed and seeds
scraped out
juice of 1 lime
1 teaspoon sugar
5gms fresh coriander
salt to taste

Place all ingredients in the **Master Prep**® Processing Bowl, onion first and coriander last. Secure the top and pulse 2-3 times for a chunky, chutney like salsa. Pulse a few times more for a smoother sauce-like salsa.

Salt to taste and serve with tortilla chips or alongside grilled chicken or fish.

✳TIP

While fresh pineapple makes a wonderful salsa, canned pineapple chunks will work fine, as long as they are drained well. Most grocery stores also sell quarts of pre-cut fresh pineapple chunks or rings in refrigerated cases in or near the produce department.

YOU'LL NEED:

✓ 1200ml Bowl
✓ Blade Assembly
✓ Bowl Lid

MARVELLOUS STUFFED MUSHROOMS

SERVES 6

15-20 large mushrooms, scrubbed
1 small shallot, peeled
2 cloves garlic, peeled
1 tablespoon fresh parsley leaves
2 teaspoons lemon juice
½ teaspoon salt
⅛ teaspoon pepper
1 tablespoon olive oil
2 tablespoons butter or margarine
3 tablespoons Parmesan cheese, grated
50gms cup Italian breadcrumbs

✳ TIP

Pulse 240gm of cream cheese, 1 tablespoon lemon juice, 1 teaspoon Old Bay seasoning and 75gms of canned lump crab meat 2-3 times and fill the mushroom caps without sautéing for an entirely different take on Stuffed Mushrooms.

Preheat oven to 375 degrees Fahrenheit, 190 degrees Celsius or Gas Mark 5. Snap stems from mushrooms to create mushroom cap cups that are ready for filling. Place removed stems into the **Master Prep®** Chopper.

Add shallot, garlic, parsley, lemon juice, salt, pepper and olive oil to the stems in the **Master Prep®** Chopper. Secure top and pulse 3-4 times until stems are minced, not mushy. Heat butter in a sauté pan over medium high heat until sizzling and then add the minced stem mixture to the pan. Sauté for 2-3 minutes until stem pieces begin to brown.

Remove stem mixture from heat and stir in Parmesan cheese and breadcrumbs until well combined. Spoon an overflowing mound of the mixture into each mushroom cap and arrange on a baking sheet, single layer. Bake for 8-10 minutes until mushrooms take on a light brown, roasted colour. Serve hot.

YOU'LL NEED:

✓ 500ml Chopper
✓ Blade Assembly
✓ Chopper Lid

QUICHE LORRAINE CUPS

SERVES 12

3 large eggs
60gms cream cheese
⅛ teaspoon white pepper
⅛ teaspoon nutmeg
¼ teaspoon salt
8 chives
4 slices bacon, cooked
100gms Swiss cheese, grated
24 mini puffed pastry or Filo dough shells, tart
cups, or 12 homemade pastry cups (see tips)

Preheat oven to 375 degrees Fahrenheit, 190 degrees Celsius or Gas Mark 5. If using thin Filo dough shells, pre-bake them for 6 minutes to crisp up before filling with quiche or they may get soggy and collapse.

Place eggs, cream cheese, white pepper, nutmeg and salt in the **Master Prep®** Chopper. Secure Chopper's top and pulse for 8-10 seconds until well combined and frothy.

Add chives and cooked bacon slices to the egg mixture and re-secure Chopper's top. Pulse 3-4 quick times to chop bacon and onion into small pieces and disperse throughout.

Arrange tart cups on a sheet pan and place a small pinch of the grated Swiss cheese at the bottom of each.

Use a small spoon to fill each tart cup with the quiche filling from the **Master Prep®** Chopper, scooping from the bottom to ensure getting bacon in each cup. Bake 10-25 minutes (times will vary greatly depending on which cups used), until tart cups are golden brown on the outside and a toothpick stuck into filling comes out clean. Let cool for 5 minutes before serving.

✳TIP

To make your own pastry cups: use prepared puffed pastry sheets (sold in a 2 pack in the frozen food aisle), unroll and cut into 3 inch rounds. Form the rounds around the inside circumference of a 12 cup muffin pan before filling with quiche filling.

YOU'LL NEED:

✓ 500ml Chopper
✓ Blade Assembly
✓ Chopper Lid

LIGHT AND FLUFFY DEVILED EGGS

SERVES 12

12 hardboiled eggs, shelled
60ml mayonnaise
60ml salad dressing
¼ teaspoon paprika
⅛ teaspoon onion powder
½ teaspoon ground mustard
¼ teaspoon salt
⅛ teaspoon pepper

✳TIP

If you like sweet relish in your deviled eggs, simply add a tablespoon after step 2 and pulse 1 quick time to combine. This is also a good time to add my personal favorite… cooked bacon.

Cut eggs in half lengthwise and remove yolks, transferring them to the **Master Prep**® Chopper.

Cover egg yolks in the **Master Prep**® Chopper with all remaining ingredients. Secure Chopper's top and pulse 15-20 seconds until the yolk filling is fluffy and smooth.

Use a spoon or pastry bag to stuff the yolk filling back into the hardboiled egg whites.

Serve garnished with an additional sprinkling of paprika over top.

YOU'LL NEED:

✓ 500ml Chopper
✓ Blade Assembly
✓ Chopper Lid

BLUE CHEESE SLIDERS

SERVES 6 TO 12 AS APPETIZERS OR 4 AS A MAIN COURSE.

A hearty appetizer or casual entrée, these sliders marry grilled onions and a bold blue cheese spread for added oomph.

Blue Cheese Spread
240ml sour cream (regular or lowfat)
240ml mayonnaise (regular or lowfat)
120gms blue cheese, crumbled
1 clove garlic, peeled
2 spring onions, chopped
pinch salt

Sliders
675gms lean ground beef
½ teaspoon salt
½ teaspoon garlic salt
½ teaspoon black pepper
12 small rolls or buns, split horizontally, toasted
12 small pieces of lettuce
12 thin slices Roma tomatoes

Blue Cheese Spread: Combine all ingredients in the bowl. Pulse until smooth. Spoon into a bowl and refrigerate until use.

Sliders: In a large bowl, lightly toss together the beef, salt, garlic salt, and pepper. Form into small patties about the 1½ inches in diameter to form a total of 12 patties. Broil or grill each to your preference.

To assemble the sliders, place a small amount of the blue cheese spread on both sides of one roll. Top with a small piece of lettuce, a beef patty and a tomato slice. Cover with the remaining half roll.

YOU'LL NEED:

✓ 1200ml Bowl
✓ Blade Assembly
✓ Bowl Lid

ROASTED TOMATO & OLIVE BRUSCHETTA

MAKES ABOUT 12 SERVINGS

Roasting brings out such sweet tomato flavours and, with the addition of garlic and basil, you can't go wrong with this inviting appetizer! Use lightly toasted French bread or sourdough baguette rounds for the base.

4 medium tomatoes, cored and quartered
2 tablespoons extra-virgin olive oil
salt and pepper to taste
1 clove garlic, peeled
40gms black olives, pitted
1 teaspoon fresh basil
French bread rounds, lightly toasted

Place the tomatoes on a baking sheet and toss with the oil. Sprinkle with salt and pepper. Bake at 350 degrees Fahenheit, 180 degrees Celsius or Gas Mark 4 for 30 to 40 minutes, or until very soft and tender. Remove and cool slightly.

Place the cooled tomatoes in the bowl and add the garlic, olives and basil. Add a few drops of oil if the mixture looks dry. Pulse for just a few seconds, or long enough to roughly chop the vegetables together. Don't over-blend.

YOU'LL NEED:

✓ 1200ml Bowl
✓ Blade Assembly
✓ Bowl Lid

CHAPTER FIVE
Soups, Bisque & Sauces

COOL AND CREAMY GAZPACHO

SERVES 2

1 Anaheim (mild) chilli pepper, seeded and cut in quarters
1 cucumber peeled and cut in quarters
2 cloves garlic, peeled
2 tablespoons balsamic vinegar
1 teaspoon salt
3 ripe tomatoes, cored and quartered
croutons, for garnish

Place chilli pepper, cucumber, garlic, balsamic vinegar and salt in the **Master Prep®** Processing Bowl. Secure top and pulse in 5-7 quick bursts until pepper and cucumber begin to break up.

Remove top and use a spoon to push mixture down, away from the walls of the Processing Bowl.

Add tomatoes, re-secure top and pulse for 5 seconds, until all ingredients are well combined, but not liquefied. Serve chilled, topped with croutons.

✳ TIP

Save even more prep time by substituting 12 cherry tomatoes for the regular tomatoes in the recipe. I like to garnish gazpacho with both the croutons and a nice sized dollop of sour cream.

YOU'LL NEED:

√ **1200ml Bowl**
√ **Blade Assembly**
√ **Bowl Lid**

ROASTED BUTTERNUT SQUASH SOUP

MAKES 6

1 butternut squash (about 900gms)
55gms baby carrots
2 tablespoons butter
720ml vegetable stock
¼ teaspoon onion powder
⅛ teaspoon ground nutmeg
⅛ teaspoon allspice
salt and pepper to taste

TIP

Garnish with a dollop of sour cream to make this soup even creamier. Skip the onion powder, add 2 tablespoons of sugar and chill before serving to make a refreshing dessert soup that is best garnished with whipped cream.

Preheat oven to 425 degrees Fahrenheit, 220 degrees Celsius or Gas Mark 7. Cut squash in half lengthwise, remove seeds and place flesh side down on a sheet pan. Bake for 35-40 minutes until flesh is extremely soft. Let cool before handling.

Use a large spoon to scoop roasted squash out of rind, placing in the **Master Prep**® Pitcher. Add carrots, secure Pitcher's top, and pulse for 8-10 seconds until squash is smooth and carrots are minced throughout.

Transfer mixture to a large stock pot over medium high heat. Cover with remaining ingredients and stir to combine. Bring up to a simmer and cook for 5 minutes.

Salt and pepper to taste and serve immediately.

YOU'LL NEED:

✓ 1500ml Pitcher
✓ Blade Assembly
✓ Pitcher Lid

RULE THE KITCHE

CREAM OF TOMATO SOUP

SERVES 2

¼ of 1 onion, peeled
2 cloves garlic, peeled
1 tablespoon fresh basil
1 tablespoon fresh parsley
2 tablespoons extra virgin olive oil
2 tomatoes, tops trimmed off and quartered
2 tablespoons tomato paste
120ml double cream
120ml chicken stock
salt and pepper to taste

Place all ingredients in the **Master Prep®** Processing Bowl. Secure Processing Bowl's top and pulse for 10 seconds in quick bursts until soup is nearly pureed.

Carefully remove blades from the **Master Prep®** Processing Bowl and microwave soup, in Processing Bowl, for 2-3 minutes, stirring halfway through.

Salt and pepper to taste and serve with Italian bread, or topped with croutons.

TIP

Substituting single cream for the double cream will keep this soup creamy without all of the fat. Try topping with a pinch of grated Parmesan cheese for a little extra flavour!

YOU'LL NEED:

✓ 1200ml Bowl
✓ Blade Assembly
✓ Bowl Lid

BROCCOLI AND CHEESE SOUP

SERVES 2

120gm processed cheese
100gms frozen broccoli florets
60gms strong Cheddar cheese
240ml chicken stock
240ml milk
½ teaspoon onion powder
¼ teaspoon white pepper
salt

TIP

I've kept this recipe small to be microwaved straight in the **Master Prep®** Processing Bowl. The ingredients in this recipe can easily be doubled to make 4 servings, but must be made in the large, **Master Prep®** Pitcher, which is not microwave safe. In that case, simply heat on the stove over medium heat, until melted and hot.

Place all ingredients in the **Master Prep®** Processing Bowl. Secure Processing Bowl's top and pulse 5 quick times until broccoli florets are chopped.

Carefully remove blades from the **Master Prep®** Processing Bowl and microwave soup, in Processing Bowl, for 2-3 minutes, stirring halfway through.

Stir well, salt to taste and serve with crusty bread for dipping.

YOU'LL NEED:

✓ **1200ml Bowl**
✓ **Blade Assembly**
✓ **Bowl Lid**

RULE THE KITCHEN

CREAM OF ASPARAGUS SOUP

SERVES 4

450gms fresh asparagus spears
2 tablespoons butter or margarine
1 shallot, peeled and diced
1 stalk celery, cut into 2 inch lengths
2 cloves garlic, peeled
480ml chicken stock
1 teaspoon lemon juice
⅛ teaspoon nutmeg
¼ teaspoon white pepper
240ml single cream
salt to taste

✳ TIP

To cook the asparagus tip garnish in no time: fill a small, microwave safe, bowl with about 2 inches of water and drop asparagus tips down into it. Microwave for about 2 minutes or until water begins to bubble. Carefully remove from microwave and retrieve asparagus tips with a fork.

Trim asparagus stalks about 2 inches up from the bottom and discard bottoms. Trim asparagus tips off remaining stalks and reserve. Finally, cut stalks in half. Heat butter in a large stock pot over medium-high heat until melted, and then add shallot, celery and garlic. Sauté until onions are clear and whole garlic cloves begin to brown.

Add chicken stock, lemon juice and asparagus stalks and bring to a boil. Once boiling, reduce to a simmer, and simmer for 15 minutes. Remove from heat, add all but 4 of the asparagus tips and let cool for 15 minutes. Place boiled asparagus and stock mixture, nutmeg and white pepper in the **Master Prep**® Pitcher. Secure the Pitcher's top and pulse for 10 seconds, until almost entirely smooth.

Return the pureed mixture to the stove and cook over medium heat, stirring in the single cream, a little at a time. Stir constantly to ensure that the soup does not boil. Cook for 4 minutes or until hot and remove from heat. Salt to taste and serve each bowl garnished with 1 of the 4 reserved asparagus tips.

YOU'LL NEED:

✓ **1500ml Pitcher**
✓ **Blade Assembly**
✓ **Pitcher Lid**

CUBAN BLACK BEAN SOUP

SERVES 4

2 cans (420gms each) black beans, drained
480ml beef stock
240ml Fresh Tomato Salsa, recipe page: 64
1 tablespoon lime juice
½ teaspoon chilli powder
1 teaspoon cumin
salt and pepper to taste
sour cream, optional, for garnish

TIP

If you like spice, you may also want to garnish with slices of fresh jalapeño and you'll certainly want to consider adding a few drops of smoked jalapeno pepper flavoured hot sauce to the soup.

Place 2/3 of the black beans, and all of the beef stock in the **Master Prep**® Pitcher. Secure Pitcher's top and pulse for about 15-20 seconds, until smooth.

Place a pot over medium high heat. Pour bean and beef stock mixture into pot and cover with remaining black beans, Fresh Tomato Salsa, lime juice, chilli powder and cumin. Bring up to a simmer and then lower heat to medium low.

Cook for 20 minutes, stirring occasionally. Salt and pepper to taste and serve hot, garnished with a dollop of sour cream.

YOU'LL NEED:

✓ **1500ml Pitcher**
✓ **Blade Assembly**
✓ **Pitcher Lid**

RULE THE KITCHE

HOMEMADE APPLE SAUCE

SERVES 6

4 large apples, peeled and cored
160ml water
2 tablespoons sugar
1 tablespoon light brown sugar
⅛ teaspoon cinnamon, optional

✳ TIP

Try making this with apple juice or cider in place of the water for a bigger, bolder apple taste. Throw a handful of fresh strawberries into the Processing Bowl in step 4 for great Strawberry Apple Sauce without the artificial flavours you'd find in the store-bought variety.

Place apples, water, sugar and brown sugar in a covered pot and heat on stove over medium heat, stirring occasionally until simmering.

Lower heat to medium low and let simmer for 10 minutes.

Remove from heat and let cool, uncovered, for 15 minutes.

Transfer apple mixture to the **Master Prep®** Processing Bowl, add cinnamon and secure the top. Pulse in quick bursts for about 1 minute or until your desired consistency has been reached. Cover and refrigerate for 1-2 hours before serving.

YOU'LL NEED:

✓ 1200ml Bowl
✓ Blade Assembly
✓ Bowl Lid

GREEK CUCUMBER SAUCE

SERVES 6

1 medium cucumber
2 cloves garlic, peeled
1 tablespoon lemon juice
1 tablespoon fresh dill
480ml plain yoghurt
salt and pepper to taste

✳ TIP

The thicker consistency of Greek yogurt works best for this sauce, so keep an eye out for it in the dairy section of your grocery store. Secretly, I like sour cream even better!

Peel cucumber, and then slice in half lengthwise. Spoon out the softer, seed filled portion in the center and discard. Quarter the peeled and cleaned cucumber halves to fit into the **Master Prep**® Chopper.

Place cucumber, garlic, lemon juice and dill in the **Master Prep**® Chopper. Secure the top and pulse 8-10 times, until well blended and cucumber is almost completely grated.

Skim any liquid off the top of yogurt, and then add to cucumber mixture in the **Master Prep**® Chopper. Re-secure the top and pulse for 10-15 seconds, until well combined. Salt and pepper to taste and then refrigerate for at least 2 hours before serving to let the flavours mingle.

YOU'LL NEED:

✓ 500ml Chopper
✓ Blade Assembly
✓ Chopper Lid

RULE THE KITCHE

FRESH BASIL PESTO

SERVES 6

40gms Parmesan cheese
3 cloves garlic, peeled
120ml extra virgin olive oil
35gms pine nuts
20gms fresh basil leaves, packed
salt and pepper to taste

TIP

If the strong flavours of pine nuts aren't for you, try substituting walnuts, cashews or blanched almonds. I like the blanched almonds best as their outer hull has been removed and won't turn your pesto brown.

Place Parmesan cheese and garlic cloves in the *Master Prep®* Chopper.

Secure top and process in one long, 30 second pulse until cheese is grated. (Skip this step if using store bought grated cheese).

Add remaining ingredients, then fresh basil leaves last and secure top.

Use 8-10 short pulses until pesto is a coarse, paste-like consistency.

Salt and pepper to taste. Serve over your favorite pasta, or use as a fresh pizza or bruschetta topping. Also great on chicken or salmon!

YOU'LL NEED:

✓ 500ml Chopper
✓ Blade Assembly
✓ Chopper Lid

RASPBERRY COULIS

SERVES 8

3 tablespoons water
70gms sugar
240gms fresh raspberries
1 tablespoon lemon juice

✳TIP

For the best presentation, use a sauce or old condiment bottle to drizzle the coulis around the plate or over top of a dessert.

Place water and sugar in a small sauce pan over medium heat, stirring until sugar has dissolved. Remove from heat.

Add raspberries to dissolved sugar and then pour entire mixture into the **Master Prep**® Chopper. Secure the top and pulse in quick bursts for about 45 seconds, until smooth.

Optional: Drain coulis through a cheesecloth to remove seeds. Serve chilled.

YOU'LL NEED:

✓ 500ml Chopper
✓ Blade Assembly
✓ Chopper Lid

NO-COOK PIZZA AND PASTA SAUCE

SERVES 4

2 cans (420gms each) diced tomatoes, drained
1 can (120gm) tomato paste
2 tablespoons olive oil
2 tablespoons Parmesan cheese
2 cloves garlic, peeled
½ teaspoon oregano
4 fresh basil leaves
1 teaspoon sugar
½ teaspoon salt

Place all ingredients in the **Master Prep®** Processing Bowl. Secure the top and pulse 5 times for a chunky sauce. Pulse a few times more for an entirely smooth sauce.

Serve on homemade pizzas or pasta.

YOU'LL NEED:

✓ 1200ml Bowl
✓ Blade Assembly
✓ Bowl Lid

EASY HOLLANDAISE SAUCE

SERVES 6

3 large egg yolks
2 tablespoons lemon juice
⅛ teaspoon cayenne pepper
¼ teaspoon salt
80gms butter, melted and hot

Place egg yolks, lemon juice, cayenne pepper and salt in the **Master Prep**® Processing Bowl. Secure top and pulse for 5 seconds until combined.

Open pour spout on top of Processing Bowl and pulse the mixture in 10 second bursts as you slowly drizzle in the butter in a thin, yarn-thick stream. Continue this process until all of the butter has been combined and sauce is thick and creamy. Serve immediately while still warm.

YOU'LL NEED:

✓ 1200ml Bowl
✓ Blade Assembly
✓ Bowl Lid

CHICKEN TORTILLA SOUP

MAKES 2 TO 3 SERVINGS

A yummy soup with rich flavour and texture!

½ large white onion, peeled and quartered
1½ cloves garlic, peeled
2 jalapeño peppers, seeded
½ red bell pepper, cored and seeded
1 teaspoons extra-virgin olive oil
120gm can crushed tomatoes
1½ tablespoons fresh coriander, chopped
(½ tablespoon is reserved for garnish)
480ml to 1440ml chicken stock
1 tablespoons fresh lime juice
½ teaspoon ground cumin
¼ teaspoon salt (or to taste)
½ teaspoon freshly ground black pepper
two 6-inch corn tortillas
130gms chicken, cooked and shredded
½ avocado, pitted, peeled, and diced
50gms Cheddar cheese, grated
35gms tortilla chips, crumbled
½ lime, cut into wedges

Place the onion, garlic, peppers and red pepper in the pitcher and pulse until chopped. Heat the oil in a stockpot over medium heat. Add the chopped vegetables, tomatoes, and 2 tablespoons of coriander. Sauté and stir for about 5 minutes, or until the vegetables soften. Add the chicken stock, juice, cumin, salt and pepper. Reduce the heat and simmer until the vegetables are tender, about 15 minutes.

Place two-thirds of the soup into the pitcher. Briefly heat the corn tortillas in a dry skillet over medium heat just until softened. Tear the tortillas into pieces, add to the pitcher and pulse until the mixture is fairly smooth and thick. Pour the blended soup back into the stockpot, stirring well to incorporate.

Divide the shredded chicken between 4 soup bowls. Ladle the hot soup into the bowls and top with diced avocado, Cheddar cheese and crumbled tortilla strips. Garnish the soup with the remaining chopped coriander and lime wedges.

YOU'LL NEED:

✓ 1500ml Pitcher
✓ Blade Assembly
✓ Pitcher Lid

HOMEMADE PIZZA SAUCE

MAKES ABOUT 420ML, OR ENOUGH FOR 2 PIZZAS

Ready to use or part baked pizza bases are readily available.

180gm can tomato paste

240ml warm water

2 cloves garlic, peeled

6 large leaves fresh basil

½ teaspoon onion powder

¼ teaspoon dried oregano

¼ teaspoon dried marjoram

½ teaspoon freshly ground black pepper

½ teaspoon salt

½ teaspoon dried red pepper flakes

Place all of the ingredients in the bowl and pulse until thoroughly combined. Adjust the seasonings to your taste and add a pinch of sugar if you want to balance the acidity of the tomatoes.

✳ TIP

Make a double-batch of this sauce and freeze half for another night. Pair it with hot pasta and a grating of fresh Parmesan, pour it over chicken breasts and bake with mozzarella cheese, the list of uses is endless!

YOU'LL NEED:

✓ 1200ml Bowl

✓ Blade Assembly

✓ Bowl Lid

SOUTH AMERICAN CHIMICHURRI SAUCE

MAKES 240ML TO 360ML

There are many versions of this classic South American accompaniment for grilled meats. This recipe is a good, solid place to start using your imagination, as you add ingredients to your taste.

1 bunch fresh parsley, cleaned, large stems removed
10 large cloves garlic, peeled
1 teaspoon salt
240ml extra-virgin olive oil

Optional ingredients:
1 small white onion, peeled and quartered
120ml white wine vinegar
½ teaspoon fresh ground pepper
1 teaspoon fresh basil, thyme or oregano or a mixture of any favorite herbs

Place the parsley, garlic, salt and oil (and optional ingredients) into the bowl and pulse until finely chopped. Serve right away or store in a covered glass dish in the refrigerator for several days.

TIP

Chimichurri Sauce is more like a pesto with a hefty garlic flavour than it is a sauce and it has become increasing popular all over the world. Try it on tender lamb chops, beef kebabs, or any simple cut of beef, pork, or chicken.

YOU'LL NEED:

✓ 1200ml Bowl
✓ Blade Assembly
✓ Bowl Lid

PEANUT DIPPING SAUCE

MAKES 360ML

This sauce is a snap to prepare and can be used with just about any vegetable or chicken dish as a way to enliven your meal. If your kids like peanut butter, they will eat just about anything dipped in this sauce.

120ml hot water
8 tablespoons crunchy peanut butter
5 tablespoons Hoisin sauce
(or substitute soy sauce)
1 tablespoon Asian red chilli paste
1 tablespoon fresh lime juice

Place all of the ingredients into the bowl and pulse until completely combined. Taste and the adjust flavours and consistency to your liking.

✳ TIP

This sauce also makes a delicious base for chicken lettuce wraps. Mince cooked chicken, add 3 to 4 tablespoons of this sauce, and wrap in crisp lettuce leaves for a wonderful appetizer or snack.

YOU'LL NEED:

✓ 1200ml Bowl
✓ Blade Assembly
✓ Bowl Lid

CLASSIC LOBSTER BISQUE

SERVES 4

Lobster Bisque is the height of elegance! Use your **Ninja® Master Prep®** to cut your prep time and eliminate major mistakes.

1 medium carrot, peeled and roughly chopped
1 medium onion, peeled and roughly chopped
1 inside stalk celery, peeled, strings removed and roughly chopped
110gms unsalted butter, divided
2 uncooked lobster tails, with shells
60ml pale dry sherry or brandy
60ml dry white wine
1440ml fish stock
1 tablespoon tomato paste
1 bay leaf
6 sprigs fresh parsley
2 stems fresh thyme
3 tablespoons white flour
180ml double cream
salt and white pepper to taste
brandy as garnish

Place the carrot, onion and celery into the pitcher and pulse until the vegetables are minced. In a heavy-bottomed soup pot, melt half the butter over medium-low heat and add the carrots, onion, celery and the lobster tails in shells. Sauté 3 to 4 minutes. Add the sherry, wine, fish stock, tomato paste and herbs and simmer the stock for 30 to 40 minutes. Remove the lobsters from the stock, remove the meat from the shells and cut into large chunks, setting aside. Strain the stock through a sieve.

In a large saucepan over medium heat, melt the remaining butter. Whisk in the flour, stirring to make a roux. Steadily, whisk in the strained lobster stock, until smoothly blended.

Transfer the soup into the pitcher, in batches as needed, and pulse smooth. Return the soup to the stockpot, add the lobster and cream and simmer, stirring frequently for 10 minutes. Adjust the seasonings, if desired. To serve, pour the soup into bowls and add a splash of brandy on top. Store any leftovers in the refrigerator.

YOU'LL NEED:

√ 1500ml Pitcher
√ Blade Assembly
√ Pitcher Lid

CHAPTER SIX

Breads & Bakery Goods

HOMESTYLE BISCUITS

SERVES 6

250gms white flour
1 tablespoon baking powder
¼ teaspoon baking soda
1 teaspoon salt
6 tablespoons butter
240ml buttermilk
Non-stick cooking spray

✳ TIP

The farther apart you arrange the biscuits before cooking, the crispier the edges will turn out. Arranging them close together like the recipe calls for will make extremely light and fluffy biscuits.

Preheat oven to 450 degrees Fahrenheit, 230 degrees Celsius or Gas Mark 8.

Place flour, baking powder, baking soda, salt and butter in the **Master Prep®** Pitcher. Secure Pitcher's top and pulse 5 quick times, just until combined, not smooth.

Add buttermilk to the flour mixture and re-secure Pitcher's top. Pulse 5 quick times, just enough to combine.

Flour a large surface and lay out finished biscuit dough. Stretch and lightly press dough down until it is well under an inch thick.

Use a round cookie cutter or the rim of a thin drink glass to cut 12 biscuits from dough. Spray sheet pan with non-stick cooking spray and arrange biscuits, huddled together and nearly touching. Bake for 18-22 minutes, until tops are golden brown.

YOU'LL NEED:

✓ 1500ml Pitcher
✓ Blade Assembly
✓ Pitcher Lid

CRANBERRY ALMOND MUFFINS

SERVES 12

110gms butter or margarine
120ml milk
2 large eggs
150gms sugar
250gms white flour
2 teaspoons baking powder
⅛ teaspoon salt
1 teaspoon vanilla extract
½ teaspoon lemon zest
70gms slivered almonds
130gms frozen cranberries

Preheat oven to 375 degrees Fahrenheit , 190 degrees Celsius or Gas Mark 5. Line a 12 cup muffin pan with paper muffin liners or grease well to bake without liners.

Place butter, milk, eggs and sugar in the **Master Prep®** Pitcher. Secure Pitcher's top and pulse for 8-10 seconds, until frothy.

Add flour, baking powder, salt, vanilla extract and lemon zest to butter and egg mixture in the **Master Prep®** Pitcher. Re-secure top and pulse for 15-20 additional seconds until batter is smooth and free of lumps.

Remove Pitcher's top, carefully remove blades and add almonds and cranberries to the batter. Use a wooden or plastic spoon to gently combine them into the batter.

Fill lined or greased muffin cups with equal amounts of batter and bake for 25-30 minutes, until a toothpick inserted into the center comes out clean. Let cool for 5 minutes before serving.

☀ TIP

If you have whole almonds in the pantry, simply give them 3 or 4 pulses in the **Master Prep®** Chopper before making the muffins to roughly chop them down to size.

YOU'LL NEED:

✓ **1500ml Pitcher**
✓ **Blade Assembly**
✓ **Pitcher Lid**

RULE THE KITCHE

BOLDLY BLUEBERRY MUFFINS

SERVES 12

110gms butter or margarine, softened
120ml milk
2 large eggs
200gms sugar
500gms white flour
2 teaspoons baking powder
⅛ teaspoon salt
1 teaspoon vanilla extract
180gms blueberries

✳TIP

Add a pinch of cinnamon to the batter for something a little different. Substitute fresh raspberries in place of the blueberries for homemade Raspberry Muffins!

Preheat oven to 375 degrees Fahrenheit, 190 degrees Celsius or Gas Mark 5. Line a 12 cup muffin pan with paper muffin liners or grease well to bake without liners. Place butter, milk, eggs and sugar in the **Master Prep®** Pitcher. Secure Pitcher's top and pulse for 8-10 seconds, until frothy.

Add flour, baking powder, salt and vanilla extract to butter and egg mixture in the **Master Prep®** Pitcher. Re-secure top and pulse for 15-20 additional seconds until batter is smooth and free of lumps.

Remove Pitcher's top, carefully remove blades and add blueberries to the batter. Use a wooden or plastic spoon to gently fold blueberries into the batter, careful not to break them and release their colour.

Fill lined or greased muffin cups with equal amounts of batter and bake for 23-28 minutes, until a toothpick inserted into the center comes out clean. Let cool for 5 minutes before serving.

YOU'LL NEED:

✓ 1500ml Pitcher
✓ Blade Assembly
✓ Pitcher Lid

BAKED MERINGUE COOKIES

SERVES 18

3 large egg whites
¼ teaspoon cream of tartar
150gms sugar
½ teaspoon vanilla extract

Preheat oven to 200 degrees Fahrenheit, 110 degrees celsius or Gas Mark 1/4 and line a baking sheet with parchment paper.

Place egg whites and cream of tartar in the **Master Prep®** Processing Bowl. Secure the top and pulse in 15 second intervals for about 90 seconds, or until egg whites are nearly strong enough to cling to an upside down spoon.

✳TIP

Use a pastry bag with various pastry tips to create unique and beautiful meringue cookies. Various extracts and food colourings may be added in step 3 to completely change their look and flavour!

Open the **Master Prep®** Processing Bowl's pour spout and pour in about ¼ of the sugar, and all of the vanilla extract. Pulse for 10 seconds, and then pour in another ¼ of the sugar. Repeat until sugar is fully combined and then pulse an additional 20 seconds. Meringue should be forming stiff peaks (that stay formed).

Use a teaspoon to spoon small, quarter sized lumps of the meringue onto a baking sheet about an inch apart. (You may have enough meringue to fill 2 baking sheets!)

Bake for 80-90 minutes, until cookies do not give when you poke them. Crack oven door and let cookies cool, in oven, for 2 hours before serving.

YOU'LL NEED:

✓ **1200ml Bowl**
✓ **Blade Assembly**
✓ **Bowl Lid**

PEANUT BUTTER COOKIES

SERVES 12

110gms butter or margarine softened
140gms peanut butter
1 large egg
400 - 600gms sugar
75gms light brown sugar
½ teaspoon vanilla extract
160gms white flour
1 teaspoon baking soda
¼ teaspoon salt

Preheat oven to 375 degrees Fahrenheit, 190 degrees Celsius or Gas Mark 5 and spray a baking sheet with non-stick cooking spray.

Place peanut butter, butter, egg, sugar, brown sugar and vanilla extract in the **Master Prep®** Pitcher. Secure top and pulse for 10 seconds, until well combined.

Add flour, baking soda and salt to the peanut butter mixture and re-secure top. Pulse for 15-20 seconds until cookie dough is smooth and lump free.

Carefully remove blades from Pitcher, and then scoop out cookie dough, one rounded tablespoon at a time. Use your palms to form into perfectly round balls, and then drop onto the greased baking sheet about 1½ inches apart. (You may have enough dough to fill two sheet pans!)

Press cookies down with a fork, first vertically, then horizontally, to create the classic, woven look of peanut butter cookies that also promotes even baking. Bake for 10 minutes for chewy cookies and 12-14 minutes for crispy. Makes about 24 cookies.

TIP

For chunky peanut butter cookies: Pulse 55gms of roasted peanuts in the **Master Prep®** Chopper, just 2-3 times until chopped. Add chopped peanuts to dough right before forming cookies, or sprinkle over top before pressing down with a fork.

YOU'LL NEED:

✓ 1500ml Pitcher
✓ Blade Assembly
✓ Pitcher Lid

CARROT CAKE

SERVES 8

165gms baby carrots
240ml vegetable oil
170gms sugar
3 large eggs
170gms flour
1½ teaspoons baking soda
¼ teaspoon salt
1 rounded teaspoon cinnamon
1 teaspoon vanilla extract
1 batch Whipped Cream Cheese Frosting, recipe
page: 151

Preheat oven to 350 degrees Fahrenheit, 180 degrees Celsius or Gas Mark 4. Place carrots in the **Master Prep®** Pitcher. Secure top and pulse for 10 seconds, until carrots are grated into tiny pieces. Remove carrots and set aside.

Place vegetable oil, sugar and eggs in **Master Prep®** Pitcher. Secure top and pulse for 10 seconds, until combined and frothy.

Add flour, baking soda, salt, cinnamon and vanilla extract to the sugar mixture in Pitcher and re-secure top. Pulse for 10 seconds until well combined and free of lumps.

Carefully remove blades from Pitcher and stir in grated carrots with a long spoon. Pour finished cake batter into two, greased and floured 8 inch cake pans. Bake for 30 minutes or until a toothpick inserted into the center comes out clean.

Let cool for at least 1 hour. Use a bread knife to slice off each half of the cake's rounded tops for a perfectly flat, bakery style cake. Frost each top with Cream Cheese Frosting, and then flip one on top of the other to let the frosting of each half glue the cake together. Frost the outside of the cake, decorate and serve.

✳TIP

I like to add 65gms raisins in step 5 to make this cake even better! To make carrot decorations: most stores sell small tubes of green and orange icing, as well as pastry tips that fit right onto the tube.

YOU'LL NEED:

✓ 1500ml Pitcher
✓ Blade Assembly
✓ Pitcher Lid

AWESOME BROWNIES

SERVES 9

165gms butter or margarine
55gms cocoa powder
150gms sugar
55gms light brown sugar
125gms flour
¾ teaspoon baking powder
2 large eggs
1 teaspoon vanilla extract
100gms pecans
95gms semi-sweet chocolate chips
Non-stick cooking spray

Preheat oven to 350 degrees Fahrenheit, 180 degrees Celsius or Gas Mark 4. Place butter in the **Master Prep**® Processing Bowl (without blades in place) and microwave on high for 45-60 seconds, until melted.

Insert blades and add cocoa powder to the melted butter. Secure top and pulse in 7 short bursts, or until well combined.

Add sugar, brown sugar, flour, baking powder, eggs, and vanilla extract to the cocoa mixture and re-secure top. Pulse in 7-10 long bursts, or until well combined and free of lumps.

Add pecans to the **Master Prep**® Chopper and secure top. Pulse in 5 short bursts, just until pecans are lightly chopped.

Carefully remove blades from Processing Bowl and stir in chopped pecans and chocolate chips with a long spoon. Pour batter into an 8x8 baking dish sprayed with non-stick cooking spray. Bake for 30-35 minutes, or until a toothpick inserted into the center comes out mostly clean. Slice into 9 squares to serve.

TIP

Walnuts can be substituted in place of the pecans, or try using peanuts and substituting peanut butter morsels in place of the chocolate chips for Peanut Butter Cup Brownies!

YOU'LL NEED:

√ **1200ml Bowl**
√ **Blade Assembly**
√ **Bowl Lid**

RULE THE KITCHEN

APPLE,
CRANBERRY &
GORGONZOLA
SALAD
P. 131

CHAPTER SEVEN

Entrées, Salads & Sides

PISTACHIO CRUSTED TILAPIA

SERVES 4

non-stick cooking spray
100gms unsalted pistachios, shelled
2 teaspoons Italian seasoning
3 tablespoons Dijon mustard
2 teaspoons honey
½ teaspoon garlic powder
½ teaspoon salt
¼ teaspoon pepper
4 tilapia fillets

✳ TIP

When shopping for tilapia, I always keep an eye out for domestic tilapia, as it is usually far better quality than those raised elsewhere.

Preheat oven to 375 degrees Fahrenheit, 190 degrees Celsius or Gas Mark 5. Spray a sheet pan with non-stick cooking spray.

Place pistachios and Italian seasoning in the **Master Prep®** Chopper. Secure Chopper's top and pulse 4-5 times until pistachios are minced small.

In a separate bowl, use a spoon to combine Dijon mustard, honey, garlic powder, salt and pepper.

Spread an even coat of the mustard sauce on the top of the tilapia fillets. Sprinkle pistachio mixture across the top of mustard and lightly press into. Place crusted tilapia fillets on greased sheet pan and bake for 10-15 minutes, until fish is flaky and crust is crunchy.

Serve over rice or with your favorite sides.

YOU'LL NEED:

✓ **500ml Chopper**
✓ **Blade Assembly**
✓ **Chopper Lid**

ITALIAN STYLE MEATBALLS

SERVES 4

450gms of beef round or shoulder roast, cut into 1 to 2 inch pieces

40gms Parmesan Herb Breadcrumbs, recipe page: 170

80ml milk

1 large egg

60gms Parmesan cheese

2 cloves garlic, peeled

1 tablespoon parsley flakes

½ teaspoon dry oregano

1 teaspoon salt

½ teaspoon ground black pepper

Place all ingredients in the **Master Prep®** Pitcher. Secure top and pulse for 10-15 seconds, until meat is ground.

Carefully remove blades from Pitcher, and then scoop out meatball mixture, one extremely rounded tablespoon at a time. Use your palms to form into perfectly round balls.

Cook using your favorite method for cooking meatballs, or bake on a greased sheet pan in a 350 degree Fahrenheit, 180 degree Celsius or Gas Mark 4 oven for about 25 minutes; until a meat thermometer registers the internal temperature has reached 160 degrees Fahrenheit or 70 degrees Celsius.

Serve over pasta with marinara sauce or on hoagie rolls with sauce and provolone cheese.

✳ TIP

For even moister meatballs, simmer them in marinara sauce for 20-30 minutes until cooked through. If sauce reduces too much, add a little bit of water to thin it out (though, you have to love a hearty tomato sauce).

YOU'LL NEED:

✓ **1500ml Pitcher**
✓ **Blade Assembly**
✓ **Pitcher Lid**

LASAGNE STYLE PENNE BAKE

SERVES 6

360gms dry penne pasta

480gms part skim ricotta cheese

60gms Parmesan cheese

100gms plus 100gms mozzarella cheese

1 large egg

1 teaspoon Italian seasoning

1 teaspoon parsley flakes

½ teaspoon salt

¼ teaspoon ground black pepper

1 batch No-Cook Pizza and Pasta Sauce, recipe page: 84

✳ TIP

About 480ml of any store bought tomato sauce can be used in place of my No-Cook Pizza and Pasta Sauce. Try adding a layer of thinly sliced zucchini and yellow squash between the cheese and pasta for a ratatouille twist.

Preheat oven to 375 degrees Fahrenheit, 190 degrees Celsius or Gas Mark 5. Boil pasta according to the directions on box. Drain and return to pot.

Place ricotta, Parmesan cheese, 100gms of the mozzarella cheese, egg, Italian seasoning, parsley flakes, salt and pepper in the **Master Prep®** Processing Bowl. Secure Processing Bowl's top and pulse 4-5 times until well combined.

Add No-Cook Pizza and Pasta Sauce to the penne pasta and stir until pasta is evenly coated.

Transfer penne pasta in sauce to a deep 8x8 or 9x9 baking dish. Remove blades from the **Master Prep®** Processing Bowl and pour cheese mixture over top of pasta, spreading it out evenly with a knife. Top with remaining 100gms of mozzarella cheese.

Place dish in oven and bake for 20-25 minutes until cheese begins to brown around the edges. Let cool for 5 minutes before serving.

YOU'LL NEED:

✓ 1200ml Bowl

✓ Blade Assembly

✓ Bowl Lid

SPINACH STUFFED PORK LOIN

SERVES 4

1 tablespoon olive oil

2 cloves garlic, peeled

20gms spinach leaves

100gms part skim ricotta cheese

1 large egg

1 teaspoon Italian seasoning

¼ teaspoon pepper

900gms boneless pork loin

salt and pepper

✳ TIP

You can also use this method to stuff pork loin with my Fresh Basil Pesto, recipe page: 82

Preheat oven to 350 degrees Fahrenheit, 180 degrees Celsius or Gas Mark 4. Grease a sheet pan with the tablespoon of olive oil.

Place garlic cloves in the **Master Prep®** Processing Bowl. Secure Processing Bowl's top and pulse 4-5 times until garlic is minced.

Add fresh spinach leaves, ricotta cheese, egg, Italian seasoning and pepper to the minced garlic and re-secure top. Pulse 2-3 times until all ingredients are combined and spinach is chopped, but not liquefied.

Use a long knife to butterfly, or slice the pork loin lengthwise, about ½ inch up from the bottom of the loin. Slice until you are about ¾ of the way deep, then unfold the meat and use the palm of your hand to flatten down the thicker side. If too thick, slice into the thick side in the same manner as the first butterfly you performed.

Spread spinach and ricotta mixture evenly across the flattened pork loin. Carefully roll the stuffed loin up like a pinwheel, making sure to push any filling back in as it may try to escape. Wrap loin in baking twine and tie off at least three times throughout the roast.

Generously season rolled and tied pork loin with salt and pepper. Place on the greased baking sheet and bake for 40-50 minutes, until a meat thermometer registers 150 degrees Fahrenheit or 65 degrees Celsius. Let cool for 5 minutes before removing twine and slicing into ½ inch slices to serve.

YOU'LL NEED:

✓ **1200ml Bowl**

✓ **Blade Assembly**

✓ **Bowl Lid**

RULE THE KITCHEN

TURKEY MEATLOAF WITH SUN-DRIED TOMATOES AND PARMESAN

SERVES 4

20gms Parmesan Herb Breadcrumbs,
recipe page: 170
60ml milk
2 cloves garlic, peeled
60gms Parmesan cheese
675gms uncooked turkey breast,
cut into 1 inch pieces
40gms sun-dried tomatoes
1 large egg
1 tablespoon olive oil
½ teaspoon salt
¼ teaspoon ground black pepper
2 tablespoons ketchup
1 tablespoon Dijon mustard

✳TIP

Store bought breadcrumbs will work fine in this recipe, but I'd suggest buying seasoned breadcrumbs for the most flavour. They should still be soaked in milk to keep the turkey meat moist.

Preheat oven to 350 degrees Fahrenheit, 180 degrees Celsius or Gas Mark 4. Soak breadcrumbs in milk for 15 minutes before preparing meatloaf.

Place garlic and Parmesan cheese (unless cheese is already grated) in the **Master Prep®** Pitcher. Secure top and pulse 5-7 times in quick bursts until garlic is minced. Add cubed turkey breast, sun-dried tomatoes, egg, olive oil, salt, pepper and breadcrumbs and milk mixture to the **Master Prep®** Pitcher. Secure top and pulse for 8-10 seconds, until meat is ground.

Carefully remove blades from Pitcher and then scoop meatloaf mixture into a loaf or bread pan. Combine ketchup and Dijon mustard to make a topping and spread over top.

Bake 50-60 minutes, or until internal temperature of meatloaf reaches 160 degrees Fahrenheit or 70 degrees Celsius. Let cool for 5 minutes before slicing. Serve over rice or with your favorite sides.

YOU'LL NEED:

✓ **1500ml Pitcher**
✓ **Blade Assembly**
✓ **Pitcher Lid**

NINJA® PIZZA

SERVES 4

1 ready to top pizza crust (such as Boboli brand)
360ml No-Cook Pizza and Pasta Sauce,
recipe page: 84
150gms mozzarella cheese
¼ of 1 red onion, peeled
75gms black olives
½ of 1 small green bell pepper
15-20 slices pepperoni
2 tablespoons Parmesan cheese

✳ TIP

Pre-baking the crust for the 5 minutes is not entirely necessary, but does give it just the right amount of crispiness. I find that baking the fully topped pizza directly on the rack for the full amount of time makes it too crunchy and too awkward to safely remove from the oven!

Preheat the oven to 450 degrees Fahrenheit, 230 degrees Celsius or Gas Mark 8. Pre-bake crust, directly on the oven rack, for 5 minutes. Transfer to a sheet pan.

Top crust with pizza sauce and then ¾ of the mozzarella cheese.

Place onion in the **Master Prep®** Chopper and pulse in 3-5 short pulses, just until chopped. Arrange over top of pizza. Repeat with black olives and then green bell pepper, pulsing each in Chopper 4-6 short pulses before arranging on pizza.

Top pizza with pepperoni slices. Cover all with the remaining ¼ of mozzarella cheese and sprinkle with Parmesan cheese.

Bake pizza on sheet pan 10-12 minutes, or until cheese is hot and bubbly. Let cool 3-5 minutes before cutting.

YOU'LL NEED:

✓ **500ml Chopper**
✓ **Blade Assembly**
✓ **Chopper Lid**

RULE THE KITCHEN

ALMOND CRUSTED CHICKEN

SERVES 4

non-stick cooking spray
95gms raw almonds
20gms breadcrumbs
2 cloves garlic, peeled
½ teaspoon paprika
¼ teaspoon onion powder
½ teaspoon salt
¼ teaspoon ground black pepper
4 thin chicken breasts
1 large egg white

✳TIP

To make a Dijon sauce to top chicken: sauté 2 tablespoons butter, 4 tablespoons Dijon mustard, 80ml dry white wine, 1 tablespoon lemon juice, 2 diced green onions, 1 teaspoon sugar and ½ teaspoon salt until hot.

Preheat oven to 400 degrees Fahrenheit, 200 degrees Celsius or Gas Mark 6. Spray a sheet pan with non-stick cooking spray.

Place almonds, breadcrumbs, garlic cloves, paprika, onion powder, salt and pepper in the **Master Prep®** Chopper. Secure Chopper's top and pulse 15-20 seconds until almonds are a well grated, breadcrumb consistency.

Transfer almond mixture to a plastic storage bag or large mixing bowl. Dip raw chicken breast in egg white and then add to almond mixture, pressing them into the almonds on all sides to thoroughly coat.

Lay coated chicken breasts flat on the greased sheet pan and bake for 20-25 minutes until internal temperature reaches 165 degrees Fahrenheit or 75 degrees Celsius.

Serve over rice or with your favorite sides.

YOU'LL NEED:

✓ **500ml Chopper**
✓ **Blade Assembly**
✓ **Chopper Lid**

PECAN CRUSTED SALMON

SERVES 4

non-stick cooking spray
50gms pecans
1½ tablespoons honey
2 tablespoons Dijon mustard
1 tablespoon water
½ teaspoon salt
4 boneless, skinless salmon fillets
(about 180gms each)

✳ TIP

For a Maple Pecan Salmon, substitute 2 tablespoons of pure maple syrup in place of the honey in this recipe. If Dijon mustard isn't your thing, try 2 tablespoons of low sodium soy sauce for a sweet and salty Asian flair.

Preheat oven to 375 degrees Fahrenheit, 190 degrees Celsius or Gas Mark 5. Spray a sheet pan with non-stick cooking spray.

Place pecans, honey, Dijon mustard, water and salt in the **Master Prep®** Chopper. Secure Chopper's top and pulse 5-7 times until pecans are minced small.

Spread an even coat of the pecan mixture across the top of each salmon fillet. Place crusted salmon fillets on greased sheet pan and bake for about 15 minutes.

Serve over rice or with your favorite sides.

YOU'LL NEED:

✓ **500ml Chopper**
✓ **Blade Assembly**
✓ **Chopper Lid**

CRACKER CRUMB MEATLOAF

SERVES 6

8 buttery crackers (such as Ritz)
½ of 1 onion, peeled
1 large egg
60ml single cream
½ teaspoon garlic powder
10gms fresh parsley
20gms Parmesan cheese
1 teaspoon salt
¼ teaspoon ground black pepper
675gms of ground beef
80ml ketchup
2 tablespoons light brown sugar
Additional crackers to top

Preheat oven to 350 degrees Fahrenheit, 180 degrees Celsius or Gas Mark 4.

Place crackers, onion, egg, single cream, garlic powder, parsley, Parmesan cheese, salt and pepper in the **Master Prep®** Chopper. Secure top and pulse for 7-10 short pulses, until onion is finely chopped.

In a large mixing bowl, combine onion mixture and ground beef and then scoop the meatloaf mixture into a loaf or bread pan.

Combine ketchup and light brown sugar to make a topping and spread over top of loaf.

Bake for 60-70 minutes, or until internal temperature of meatloaf reaches 160 degrees Fahrenheit or 70 degrees Celsius. Let cool for 5 minutes before slicing. Crumble additional crackers over top of ketchup layer before serving.

✳TIP

You can also make your own ground beef in the **Ninja® Master Prep®** to start this recipe. Chunks of round or chuck roast work best, but you can even use inexpensive (and already chunked) stew meat.

YOU'LL NEED:

√ **500ml Chopper**
√ **Blade Assembly**
√ **Chopper Lid**

GROUND SIRLOIN STUFFED PEPPERS

SERVES 4

4 bell peppers
450gms sirloin steak
1 onion, peeled and quartered
175gms chopped tomatoes (canned)
150gms cooked rice
½ teaspoon allspice
1 teaspoon salt
½ teaspoon ground black pepper
50gms Cheddar cheese, grated

✳ TIP

Save the tops of the bell peppers in step 1 and bake them on the sheet pan alongside the stuffed peppers to place back on top for a beautiful serving presentation.

Preheat the oven to 350 degrees Fahrenheit, 180 degrees Celsius or Gas Mark 4. Cut tops off bell peppers and scrape out seeds and membranes.

Place sirloin steak and onion in the **Master Prep**® Processing Bowl. Secure Processing Bowl's top and pulse for 8-10 seconds, until sirloin is ground and onions are finely minced throughout.

Transfer sirloin mixture to a sauté pan over medium high heat. Saute 5 minutes until sirloin begins to brown and fat cooks out.

Drain meat mixture and stir in remaining ingredients, except for the Cheddar cheese. Spoon the finished meat stuffing into the 4 hollowed out bell peppers. Top with a large pinch of Cheddar cheese.

Bake on a sheet pan, covered with aluminium foil, for about 40 minutes, until peppers are tender to the touch.

YOU'LL NEED:

✓ 1200ml Bowl
✓ Blade Assembly
✓ Bowl Lid

RULE THE KITCHE

SWEDISH MEATBALLS

SERVES 4

1 slice white bread

80ml milk

450gms beef round or shoulder roast, cut into 1 to 2 inch pieces

1 large egg

1½ tablespoons parsley flakes

½ teaspoon onion powder

⅛ teaspoon nutmeg

⅛ teaspoon allspice

1 teaspoon salt

½ teaspoon pepper

480ml sour cream

240ml beef stock

¼ teaspoon white pepper

✳ TIP

For something different: I like Swedish Meatballs served alongside gnocchi (Italian potato dumplings) rather than mashed potatoes.

Preheat oven to 350 degrees Fahrenheit, 180 degrees Celsius or Gas Mark 4.

Soak white bread in milk for 15 minutes prior to making meatballs.

Place white bread and milk, beef pieces, egg, parsley flakes, onion powder, nutmeg, allspice, salt and pepper in the *Master Prep®* Processing Bowl. Secure top and pulse for 10-15 seconds, until meat is ground.

Carefully remove blades from Processing Bowl, and then scoop out meatball mixture, one extremely rounded tablespoon at a time. Use your palms to form into perfectly round balls.

Bake on a greased sheet pan for about 25 minutes; until a meat thermometer registers the internal temperature has reached 160 degrees Fahrenheit or 70 degrees Celsius.

While meatballs are baking, prepare the gravy by adding sour cream, beef stock and white pepper to a sauce pot over medium heat. Bring up to a simmer and cook for 5 minutes, stirring constantly.

Serve meatballs alongside mashed potatoes, and smothered in gravy.

YOU'LL NEED:

✓ **1200ml Bowl**

✓ **Blade Assembly**

✓ **Bowl Lid**

CONFETTI COLESLAW

SERVES 12

240ml mayonnaise
120ml buttermilk
60ml milk
2 tablespoons vinegar
70gms sugar
½ teaspoon onion powder
½ teaspoon garlic powder
1 teaspoon celery salt
½ teaspoon ground black pepper
1 head cabbage
6 baby carrots

✳ TIP

To make an Apple Walnut Coleslaw: substitute cider vinegar in place of the white vinegar and add 1 peeled and cored apple to the **Master Prep**® Pitcher in step 2. Pulse 45gms of walnuts separately in the **Master Prep**® Pitcher, just 2-3 times until chopped. Sprinkle chopped walnuts over slaw just before serving.

Place mayonnaise, buttermilk, milk, vinegar, sugar, onion powder, garlic powder, celery salt, and ground black pepper in a large mixing bowl and stir to make the dressing.

Place baby carrots in the **Master Prep**® Pitcher.

Remove outermost leaves from cabbage and discard. Cut head of cabbage into eighths and place into the **Master Prep**® Pitcher. Secure Pitcher's top and pulse 5-7 quick times until cabbage and carrots are finely chopped. (Depending on the size of cabbage, you may need to pulse in two batches).

Transfer chopped cabbage and carrots to the large mixing bowl with dressing mixture. Mix well to combine.

Refrigerate for 1 hour to let the flavours mingle before serving.

YOU'LL NEED:

✓ **1500ml Pitcher**
✓ **Blade Assembly**
✓ **Pitcher Lid**

ROASTED GARLIC SMASHED CAULIFLOWER

SERVES 4

1 small head cauliflower
6 cloves roasted garlic, peeled (see tips)
60gms Parmesan cheese
3 tablespoons butter, softened
2 teaspoons parsley flakes
salt and pepper to taste

TIP

To roast garlic: preheat the oven to 400 degrees Fahrenheit, 200 degrees Celsius or Gas Mark 6 and line a baking sheet with foil. Lay garlic cloves out in a single layer and cover with another sheet of aluminium foil. Bake for 15-20 minutes until cloves turn a golden brown. The peel is always easier to remove after roasting.

Chop cauliflower into large florets, only disposing of the toughest stalks; boil for 6 minutes, until very soft.

Drain cauliflower extremely well and place in the **Master Prep®** Pitcher while still hot. Add remaining ingredients and secure the Pitcher's top.

Pulse for 10-15 seconds, until cauliflower is creamy and nearly smooth.

Salt and pepper to taste and serve immediately. If the smash has cooled, transfer to a microwave safe dish and microwave for 1 minute to reheat.

YOU'LL NEED:

✓ **500ml Chopper**
✓ **Blade Assembly**
✓ **Chopper Lid**

REFRIED KIDNEY BEANS

SERVES 6

2 cans (240gm) red kidney beans, drained and rinsed
2 tablespoons vegetable oil
1 small onion, peeled and quartered
1 tomato, top trimmed off and quartered
½ teaspoon cumin
¼ teaspoon coriander
1 teaspoon salt

Place all the ingredients in the **Master Prep**® Processing Bowl. Secure the top and pulse 5-7 times until combined, but chunky.

Carefully remove blades from the **Master Prep**® Processing Bowl and microwave for 2 minutes, stirring halfway through. Serve hot.

YOU'LL NEED:

✓ 1200ml Bowl
✓ Blade Assembly
✓ Bowl Lid

REALLY CREAMED CORN

SERVES 4

1 bag (600gm) frozen corn kernels, thawed
2 tablespoons butter
120ml double cream cream
60ml milk
¼ teaspoon vanilla extract
1½ tablespoons sugar
½ teaspoon salt

Place half of the corn kernels in the **Master Prep®** Processing Bowl. Pulse for 10 seconds, until pureed.

Heat butter, pureed corn, and remaining whole corn kernels in a sauce pan over medium high heat, until sizzling.

Stirring constantly, add in remaining ingredients. Reduce heat to low and simmer 2 minutes. Serve hot.

YOU'LL NEED:

✓ **1200ml Bowl**
✓ **Blade Assembly**
✓ **Bowl Lid**

SOUTHERN CORNBREAD MUFFINS

SERVES 12

non-stick cooking spray
125gm white flour
125gms cornmeal
1 large egg
240ml milk
4 tablespoons butter, softened
3 teaspoons baking powder
70gms sugar
1 teaspoon salt

Preheat oven to 350 degrees Fahrenheit, 180 degrees Celsius or Gas Mark 4. Spray a 12 cup muffin pan with non-stick cooking spray.

Place all ingredients in the **Master Prep®** Pitcher. Secure Pitcher's top and pulse for 8-10 seconds, until well mixed and free of lumps.

Fill greased muffin cups with equal amounts of batter and bake for 15-20 minutes, until a toothpick inserted into the center comes out clean. Let cool for 5 minutes before serving.

TIP

To make corn filled corn muffins, cut the milk down to 120ml and add 120ml of creamed corn. Or try cheesy corn muffins by adding a large pinch of grated Cheddar cheese to the top of each muffin in the muffin pan before baking.

YOU'LL NEED:

✓ **1500ml Pitcher**
✓ **Blade Assembly**
✓ **Pitcher Lid**

RULE THE KITCHEN

YUKON GOLD MASHED POTATOES

SERVES 6

6 Yukon gold potatoes, cubed, skin on
2 cloves garlic, peeled
60ml sour cream
3 tablespoons milk
½ teaspoon onion powder
5gms fresh parsley leaves
salt and pepper to taste

✳TIP

Whether you are using the **Ninja® Master Prep®** or not; here are two great ways to salvage the gluey consistency of over-mashed, mashed potatoes. 1. Boil an extra potato worth of potato cubes and reserve to mash in if things go wrong. 2. Stir in boxed potato flakes a tablespoon at a time until the starchiness returns.

Boil cubed potatoes for 8-10 minutes, until tender.

Drain potatoes extremely well and place in the **Master Prep®** Pitcher while still hot. Add remaining ingredients and secure the Pitcher's top.

Pulse only 3-4 times, removing top to check their consistency. Over processing will disintegrate their starch and make them very sticky. Re-secure top and pulse until your desired consistency has been reached, only pulsing in quick bursts and stopping to check for texture each time.

Salt and pepper to taste and serve with butter, sour cream and chives, or gravy. If potatoes have cooled, transfer to a microwave safe dish and microwave for 1-2 minutes, until hot.

YOU'LL NEED:

✓ **1500ml Pitcher**
✓ **Blade Assembly**
✓ **Pitcher Lid**

TWICE BAKED SWEET POTATOES

SERVES 4

4 sweet potatoes, skin on
120ml double cream
60ml milk
3 tablespoons butter
1 tablespoon maple syrup
½ teaspoon cinnamon
¼ teaspoon salt
50gms pecans
1 tablespoon light brown sugar

TIP

For the best looking Twice Baked Potatoes, pipe the filling back into the potato skins using a pastry bag and pastry tip.

Preheat oven to 400 degrees Fahrenheit, 200 degrees Celsius or Gas Mark 6, line a sheet pan with aluminum foil and bake sweet potatoes on the second to lowest rack for about 50 minutes, or until fork tender. Let potatoes cool for 10 minutes.

Slice potatoes in half lengthwise and scoop out flesh, transferring it into the **Master Prep®** Processing Bowl. Leave just about ⅓ of an inch of flesh behind in the potato skin so that skins stay somewhat sturdy.

Add double cream, milk, butter, maple syrup, cinnamon and salt to the potatoes in the **Master Prep®** Processing Bowl. Secure Processing Bowl's top and pulse for 10 seconds, until all ingredients are combined and smooth.

Carefully remove blades from Processing Bowl and use a large spoon to spoon equal amounts of the pureed potato back into the potato skins.

Place pecans and brown sugar in the **Master Prep®** Chopper. Secure top and pulse 3-5 times, until pecans are chopped. Sprinkle mixture over top of the potatoes. Bake potatoes for an additional 10 minutes until filling hardens slightly. Serve hot.

YOU'LL NEED:

✓ **1200ml Bowl**
✓ **Blade Assembly**
✓ **Bowl Lid**

POTATO PANCAKES

SERVES 4

3 large potatoes, peeled and quartered
¼ of 1 onion, peeled
1 large egg
1 teaspoon lemon juice
2 tablespoons white flour
¼ teaspoon baking powder
2 teaspoons parsley flakes
¼ teaspoon pepper
3 tablespoons vegetable oil
salt to taste

✳TIP

Traditionally, potato pancakes are often served with apple sauce, which you can also prepare in the **Ninja® Master Prep®** by following the recipe on page: 80

Place all ingredients in the **Master Prep®** Processing Bowl. Secure Processing Bowl's top and pulse for 5-10 seconds, until all ingredients are finely minced and clumping together.

Heat oil in a large sauté pan over medium high heat. Spoon rounded tablespoons of the potato pancake batter into pan and fry 2-3 minutes on each side, until golden brown. Repeat until batter is depleted.

Salt to taste while still hot and serve hot or cold.

YOU'LL NEED:

✓ **1200ml Bowl**
✓ **Blade Assembly**
✓ **Bowl Lid**

EXTRA CREAMY EGG SALAD

SERVES 4

6 hardboiled eggs, shelled
80ml mayonnaise
1 tablespoon yellow mustard
1 tablespoon butter or margarine, softened
¼ teaspoon celery salt
¼ teaspoon ground black pepper
1 tablespoon sweet relish

Separate hardboiled egg whites from yolks by slicing in half and scooping out yolks.

Place all egg yolks, mayonnaise, yellow mustard, butter, celery salt and pepper in the **Master Prep**® Chopper. Pulse 5-7 times until yolks are pulverized.

Add egg whites and sweet relish to yolk mixture and re-secure top. Pulse just 2-3 times until whites are chopped to your desired consistency.

YOU'LL NEED:

✓ **1200ml Bowl**
✓ **Blade Assembly**
✓ **Bowl Lid**

RULE THE KITCHE

HAM SALAD

SERVES 4

¼ of 1 onion, peeled
350gms cooked ham
120ml mayonnaise
1 teaspoon Worcestershire sauce
2 tablespoons sweet relish

Place all ingredients in the **Master Prep®** Processing Bowl, onion at the bottom and sweet relish on top. Secure the top and pulse in quick bursts for about 5 seconds, until your desired consistency has been reached.

Serve in sandwiches or pulse extra fine and serve as a spread on crackers or mini toasts.

YOU'LL NEED:

✓ 1200ml Bowl
✓ Blade Assembly
✓ Bowl Lid

YOUR CHOICE CHICKEN SALAD

SERVES 4

1 stalk celery, cut into 4 lengths
260gms cooked chicken pieces
25gms walnuts, shelled
120ml mayonnaise
½ teaspoon salt
⅛ teaspoon ground black pepper
¼ teaspoon onion powder
50gms cup red grapes

Place all ingredients in the **Master Prep**® Processing Bowl, celery at the bottom and grapes on top.

Secure the top and pulse in quick bursts for about 5 seconds, until your desired consistency.

Serve in sandwiches, pitta pockets, wraps or over a spinach salad garnished with diced apple and bleu cheese.

TIP

Dried cranberries make a great substitute for the grapes in this chicken salad for something a little different. Most grocery stores sell precooked "short cut" grilled chicken strips in their refrigerated cases, but I prefer to buy one of the store's whole rotisserie chickens from the deli when making chicken salad.

YOU'LL NEED:

✓ **1200ml Bowl**
✓ **Blade Assembly**
✓ **Bowl Lid**

RULE THE KITCHE

CHOPPED SALAD

SERVES 4

1 bag salad mix
½ of 1 small red onion
8-10 slices bacon, cooked
120gms strong Cheddar cheese
2 tomatoes, seeded
225gms broccoli florets

TIP

Remove most of the broccoli's stems before chopping for best results. The stronger the Cheddar cheese, the better your results will be… as harder cheeses grate better.

Place salad mix in a large serving bowl.

Cut onion, broccoli florets, tomatoes, and Cheddar cheese into large, evenly sized chunks.

Place onion in the **Master Prep®** Chopper and pulse in 3-5 short pulses, just until chopped. Arrange in a thin line atop the salad. Repeat with the bacon, pulsing in the Chopper in 4-5 short pulses and then adding to the salad. Repeat with the Cheddar cheese, pulsing in the Chopper in 5-6 short pulses and then adding to the salad.

Place tomatoes in the **Master Prep®** Processing Bowl and pulse just 2-3 short pulses, just until chopped. Arrange in another thin line atop the salad. Repeat with the broccoli florets, pulsing in the Processing Bowl just 2-3 short pulses and then adding to the salad.

YOU'LL NEED:

✓ 1200ml Bowl
✓ Blade Assembly
✓ Bowl Lid

STEAK AND CHEESE BURGERS

SERVES 4

450gms sirloin steak, cut into 1 to 2 inch chunks
1½ teaspoons Montreal steak seasoning
120gms Cheddar cheese, cut into 1 inch cubes
hamburger buns and fixings, optional

✳ TIP

This can be done with any cheese, though I prefer a medium Cheddar cheese. Stronger Cheddar cheese does not melt up as gooey. Try with Swiss or even bleu cheese! Or try mixing cheese right into your next meatloaf!

Place sirloin chunks and Montreal steak seasoning in the **Master Prep®** Processing Bowl. Secure Processing Bowl's top and pulse for 10-15 seconds, until meat is ground.

Add Cheddar cheese to the ground sirloin and re-secure the Processing Bowl's top. Pulse 3-5 times to chop and combine the cheese into the meat, leaving about ¼ inch chunks of cheese throughout.

Carefully remove blades from Processing Bowl, and then scoop out the ground sirloin and cheese, one handful at a time. Use your palms to form into patties. Makes 4 quarter pound patties.

Grill, pan fry or broil burgers as you normally would. Some cheese will almost certainly explode out of these burgers as you cook; making thicker, rather than wider patties is recommended to keep the most intact. If pan frying or boiling, thick burgers will take around 5-6 minutes to cook well on each side. Be sure to scrape any cheese from the pan into the bun with the burger!

Serve on large hamburger buns, topped with your favorite fixings.

YOU'LL NEED:

✓ 1200ml Bowl
✓ Blade Assembly
✓ Bowl Lid

SALMON BURGERS

SERVES 4

450gms raw salmon fillets, boneless and skinless
½ onion, peeled and sliced in half again
60ml tartar sauce
2 teaspoons lemon juice
2 tablespoons breadcrumbs
½ teaspoon salt
¼ teaspoon fresh black pepper
hamburger buns and fixings, optional

Place salmon fillets, onion, tartar sauce, lemon juice, breadcrumbs, salt and pepper in the **Master Prep®** Processing Bowl. Secure Processing Bowl's top and pulse for about 10 seconds, until salmon is well ground and onions are well minced.

Carefully remove blades from Processing Bowl, and then scoop out the ground salmon, one handful at a time. Use your palms to form into patties. Makes 4 quarter pound patties.

Grill, pan fry or broil burgers as you would a hamburger. Grilling or pan frying ½ inch thick patties should take about 5 minutes on each side.

Serve topped with additional tartar sauce on a hamburger bun or wheat toast with lettuce and tomato or your favorite fixings.

✳TIP

This recipe also makes a great salmon cake appetizer for a party or get together, in place of the more typical crab cakes. Simply triple the amount of breadcrumbs added and form into small, 2 inch round cakes. Bake on a sheet pan at 400 degrees Fahrenheit, 200 degrees Celsius or Gas Mark 6.

YOU'LL NEED:

✓ **1200ml Bowl**
✓ **Blade Assembly**
✓ **Bowl Lid**

REALLY VEGGIE BURGERS

SERVES 4

1 can (450gm) garbanzo beans, drained

1 large egg

¼ of 1 onion, peeled

10gms fresh spinach

35gms mushrooms

40gms panko breadcrumbs

1 tablespoon white flour

2 teaspoons vegetable oil

½ packet powdered ranch salad dressing mix

wheat buns and fixings, optional

Place garbanzo beans, egg, onion, spinach, mushrooms, breadcrumbs, flour, vegetable oil and ranch salad dressing mix in the **Master Prep**® Processing Bowl. Secure Processing Bowl's top and pulse for about 10 seconds, until garbanzo beans are mashed and onions are well minced.

Carefully remove blades from Processing Bowl, and then scoop out the mixture, one handful at a time. Use your palms to form into patties. Makes 4 patties.

Pan fry burgers over medium high heat in a non-stick pan greased with vegetable oil or a good amount of non-stick cooking spray. Fry until lightly browned, about 5 minutes on each side.

Serve on a wheat bun with you favorite fixings.

TIP

For even crispier veggie burgers, dip the patties in additional panko breadcrumbs before pan frying. 50gms of drained, canned black beans can be added to the mixture right before forming the patties for a little bit more texture.

YOU'LL NEED:

✓ 1200ml Bowl

✓ Blade Assembly

✓ Bowl Lid

TURKEY BURGERS

SERVES 4

450gms uncooked turkey breast,
cut into 1 inch pieces
¼ of 1 onion, peeled
2 cloves garlic, peeled
2 tablespoons panko breadcrumbs
1 tablespoon soy sauce
2 tablespoons ketchup
2 teaspoons parsley flakes
½ teaspoon ground black pepper
wheat buns and fixings, optional

TIP

Ground turkey breast tends to get dry, but these burgers are pretty moist. To make them even moister, try adding 1 small zucchini after step 1, pulsing about 8 times to finely chop it into the meat.

Place turkey breast, onion, garlic, breadcrumbs, soy sauce, ketchup, parsley flakes and pepper in the ***Master Prep®*** Processing Bowl. Secure Processing Bowl's top and pulse for about 15-20 seconds, until turkey is well ground.

Carefully remove blades from Processing Bowl, and then scoop out the ground turkey, one handful at a time. Use your palms to form into patties. Makes 4 quarter pound patties.

Grill, pan fry or broil burgers as you would a hamburger. Grilling or pan frying ½ inch thick patties should take about 6 minutes on each side. Use a meat thermometer to be sure that the internal temperature reaches 165 degrees Fahrenheit or 75 degrees Celsius.

Serve on wheat buns with lettuce and tomato or your favorite fixings.

YOU'LL NEED:

✓ 1200ml Bowl
✓ Blade Assembly
✓ Bowl Lid

APPLE, CRANBERRY & GORGONZOLA SALAD

SERVES 4

Refreshing and appealing! Perfect when serving fish
or chicken as your entrée.

2 large red apples, cored and roughly chopped
1 medium cucumber, peeled and roughly cut
45gms walnuts, halved
130gms dried cranberries
90gms gorgonzola cheese, crumbled
120ml sour cream
55gms cream cheese
2 tablespoons milk
pinch salt
pinch black pepper
1 large cucumber, thinly sliced horizontally

Place the apples in the pitcher and pulse until
chopped. Remove the apples and place in a mixing
bowl. Place the cucumber and walnuts in the pitcher.
Pulse for a few seconds until roughly chopped.
Remove and add to the apples. Add the dried
cranberries and toss. Set aside.

Place the cheese, sour cream, cream cheese, milk, salt
and pepper in the pitcher. Pulse until mostly smooth.
Remove and set aside.

To serve, form the long slices of cucumber into
circular shapes and use a wooden pick to secure. Place
each on a salad plate. Fill the cucumber cups with the
apple, cucumber mixture and top each salad with the
gorgonzola salad dressing.

YOU'LL NEED:

✓ 1500ml Pitcher
✓ Blade Assembly
✓ Pitcher Lid

CHAPTER EIGHT

Marinades, Rubs & Mopping Sauces

TERIYAKI GRILLING MARINADE

MAKES ABOUT 500ML

After removing the meat from this marinade, pour the marinade into a saucepan, bring to a boil, and simmer for 5 minutes, making a luscious sauce for your grilled masterpiece.

2 cloves garlic, peeled
2 tablespoons fresh ginger, peeled and roughly chopped
¼ white onion, peeled
5gms fresh coriander, stemmed
180ml soy sauce
120ml rice wine vinegar
2 teaspoons Asian chile paste
1 tablespoon honey
2 tablespoons fresh lime juice
¾ teaspoon toasted sesame oil

Place the garlic, ginger, onion and coriander into the pitcher and pulse until uniformly chopped. Add the remaining ingredients and pulse until mixed well, but with a slightly chunky consistency. Add a little chicken stock or water to thin, if desired.

✳TIP

Pour this marinade into a self-sealing plastic bag and add a 675gms beef flank steak. Seal and marinate for 24 hours. Remove the steak, pat dry and grill for about 8 minutes per side over medium-high heat. Let rest for 5 minutes, then slice thinly across the grain. The result? Perfectly tender and flavourful teriyaki steak!

YOU'LL NEED:

✓ 1500ml Pitcher
✓ Blade Assembly
✓ Pitcher Lid

SMOKING SMOKED JALAPENO PEPPER SAUCE

MAKES ABOUT 200ML

A smoked jalapeno pepper is a dried, smoked jalapeño pepper with a spicy, smoky, slightly sweet flavour. It is often canned in a vinegary sauce called adobo. Add smoked jalapeno peppers to stews, soups, sauces and salsas. Use it sparingly until you determine how much "fire" you want to add to your favorite foods!

3 smoked jalapeno peppers, canned in adobo sauce, or less if a milder sauce is desired
1 tablespoon adobo sauce from canned smoked jalapeno peppers
4 cloves garlic, peeled
2 oranges, peeled and pulled into quarters
1 lime, juiced
1 tablespoon tomato paste
2 tablespoons apple cider vinegar
1 tablespoon extra virgin olive oil
1 teaspoon ground cumin (or more to taste)
1 teaspoon Mexican oregano
½ teaspoon salt
½ teaspoon freshly ground black pepper

Place all ingredients into the pitcher and pulse until smooth. Transfer to a medium sauce pan, over medium heat and bring to a boil. Reduce the heat to medium-low and simmer, stirring frequently, for 5 to 10 minutes. Thin with a little water if necessary. Cover and store in the refrigerator until use.

✳ TIP

All of the citrus acid in this recipe – oranges, lime, and apple cider vinegar – combine to tenderize meat perfectly. You can use this sauce alongside your favorite grilled meat, or pour the sauce into a self-sealing plastic bag with beef, chicken or pork before grilling and marinate it for a few hours.

YOU'LL NEED:

✓ 1500ml Pitcher
✓ Blade Assembly
✓ Pitcher Lid

LEMON & HERB MARINADE

MAKES ABOUT 200ML

This marinade also works beautifully as a tangy fresh salad dressing.

2 lemons, juiced (4 to 6 tablespoons)
180ml extra-virgin olive oil
1 tablespoon fresh thyme leaves
1 small sprig fresh parsley
1 small piece fresh oregano
½ teaspoon salt
½ teaspoon freshly ground black pepper

Place all ingredients into the pitcher and pulse until smooth. Taste and adjust the flavours to your liking. Use right away or cover and store in the refrigerator. If chilled, let stand at room temperature for 10 minutes to allow the oil to liquefy before serving.

TIP

Makes a light marinade for white fish fillets. Marinate the fish in the refrigerator for no more than one hour. Broil or grill and serve with lemon slices.

YOU'LL NEED:

✓ 1500ml Pitcher
✓ Blade Assembly
✓ Pitcher Lid

ORANGE PAPAYA SHRIMP MARINADE

SERVES 4 TO 6

A fruity marinade with a spicy Asian twist. Serve fabulous char-grilled shrimp over a bed of aromatic jasmine rice.

1 medium papaya, peeled and quartered
1 medium orange, peeled and pulled into quarters
2 limes, juiced
2 spring onions, cleaned, root end removed
2 tablespoons fresh basil leaves
180ml soy sauce
240ml water
2 tablespoons honey
½ teaspoon Five Spice Powder (or more to taste)
900gms fresh shrimp, deveined and cleaned, tails removed

Pulse the papaya and orange in the pitcher until roughly chopped. Add the remaining ingredients, except the shrimp, and pulse until the marinade is well combined and semi-smooth. Taste and adjust the flavours and consistency, if desired. Pour the marinade over the shrimp in a self-sealing plastic bag. Seal and refrigerate for at least 30 minutes or longer for a more intense flavour. Discard the marinade and place the shrimp on skewers. Grill the shrimp skewers for about 3 minutes per side. Makes about 350ml of marinade.

YOU'LL NEED:

✓ 1500ml Pitcher
✓ Blade Assembly
✓ Pitcher Lid

RULE THE KITCHEN

KANSAS CITY BBQ SAUCE

MAKES ABOUT 700ML

Kansas City, Missouri is considered by many to be the barbeque capitol of America. No wonder with over 100 barbecue restaurants in the city!

240ml ketchup
60ml apple cider vinegar
¼ medium white onion, peeled
2 cloves garlic, peeled
240ml tomato sauce
55gms brown sugar, packed
2 tablespoons molasses
2 tablespoons fresh lemon juice
1½ teaspoons smoked paprika
1 teaspoon freshly ground black pepper
½ teaspoon red chile powder
½ teaspoon salt

Place the ketchup, vinegar, onion and garlic into the pitcher and pulse until smooth. Add the remaining ingredients and continue to pulse until the sauce is semi-smooth.

Transfer the sauce to a medium saucepan and simmer, stirring occasionally, over low heat for 20 minutes, or until the sauce reduces by one-third. Cover and store in the refrigerator.

✳ TIP

For smoking, for grilling, for marinating, for barbeque beans – this sauce does it all!

YOU'LL NEED:

✓ 1500ml Pitcher
✓ Blade Assembly
✓ Pitcher Lid

GREEK HERB RUB

MAKES 420ML

Bring the Mediterranean into your kitchen with this very aromatic rub! It is wonderful on all meats and fish, and especially on roast lamb.

10gms oregano
10gms dried thyme
5gms dried parsley
5gms dried marjoram
1 tablespoon dried dill (optional)
1 teaspoon freshly ground black pepper
½ teaspoon salt
60ml extra virgin olive oil

Place all ingredients, except the olive oil, into the pitcher and pulse for 10 to 20 seconds. Transfer the herbs to a mixing bowl, add oil and toss to just coat the spices. Use right away or store in an airtight pitcher, in a dark, dry area, for up to 6 months.

✳TIP

It's best to let this rub sit for at least 6 to 8 hours before using. This will allow the flavours to marry into each other and the oil will be better absorbed. Slather it over any cut prior to grilling for a fabulous treat.

YOU'LL NEED:

✓ 1500ml Pitcher
✓ Blade Assembly
✓ Pitcher Lid

SWEET PAPRIKA RUB

MAKES 180ML

A fragrant and flavourful dry rub for a roast chicken or turkey that also creates tasty drippings for gravy.

110gms firmly packed brown sugar
2 tablespoons sweet paprika
2 teaspoons onion powder
2 teaspoons dry mustard
1 teaspoon crushed red pepper
½ teaspoon salt
½ teaspoon garlic powder
½ teaspoon celery seed

Place all ingredients into the pitcher and pulse for 10 seconds, until the spices and sugar are well combined. Use right away or store in an airtight pitcher, in a dark, dry area, for up to 6 months.

TIP

Smoked Hungarian sweet paprika is a specialty food item, however you can usually find it in kitchen shops, or in the ethnic food aisle of your grocery store. You can also order it easily online from various outlets. Sweet paprika opens up an entirely new flavour dimension versus the tinned ground paprika we typically use. Once you try sweet paprika, you'll probably never reach for that old tin again.

YOU'LL NEED:

✓ 1500ml Pitcher
✓ Blade Assembly
✓ Pitcher Lid

COWBOY MOPPING SAUCE

MAKES ABOUT 500ML

A thinner sauce than most marinades or barbeque sauces, mopping sauce got its name from the small slathering "mops" used for basting the meat during cooking. The purpose of a mopping sauce is to keep meat moist and add flavour during grilling. Due to the low sugar content it is not prone to burn.

¼ small white onion, peeled
2 cloves fresh garlic, peeled
120ml white wine vinegar
330ml can regular lager
1 lemon, juiced
2 teaspoons Dijon mustard
½ teaspoon freshly ground black pepper
½ teaspoon salt
½ teaspoon ground paprika
½ teaspoon cayenne pepper

Place the onion, garlic and vinegar into the pitcher and pulse, cleaning the pitcher with a spatula as needed, until finely chopped. Add the remaining ingredients and continue processing until smooth. Use right away or cover and store in refrigerator.

✳TIP

Perfect for guys who like the thrill of the grill, this sauce is great for multiple bastings as the meat cooks. Use it liberally!

YOU'LL NEED:

✓ 1500ml Pitcher
✓ Blade Assembly
✓ Pitcher Lid

BALSAMIC GRILLING SAUCE

MAKES ABOUT 360ML

This delicious sauce will create a tasty char on grilled meat.

2 tablespoons olive oil
1 large shallot, peeled and minced
240ml balsamic vinegar
180ml ketchup
2 tablespoons brown sugar
1 tablespoon garlic mustard
½ teaspoon salt
½ teaspoon freshly ground black pepper

Heat the oil in a small saucepan over medium heat; add the shallot and sauté, stirring frequently. When fragrant and soft, add the remaining ingredients, stirring well to combine. Reduce the heat to medium-low and simmer for 10 to 15 minutes. Transfer the sauce to the pitcher and pulse until smooth. Use or cover and store in refrigerator.

TIP

Substitute small sweet onions or spring onions if you don't have shallots on hand. The onion flavour blends well with the distinctive balsamic vinegar in this special sauce.

YOU'LL NEED:

✓ 1500ml Pitcher
✓ Blade Assembly
✓ Pitcher Lid

RULE THE KITCHEN

FRESH FIG SAUCE

MAKES ABOUT 360GMS

A classic combination, fresh figs and balsamic vinegar, produce an extraordinary topping for grilled meats or sumptuous desserts. There is nothing like fresh figs, but dried figs substitute beautifully if fresh are not available.

10 fresh or dried black mission figs
120ml balsamic vinegar
80ml white wine
80ml brandy
60ml orange juice
180ml water
2 tablespoons honey
½ teaspoon ground cardamom (optional)
55gms butter

Wash and de-stem the figs if using fresh fruit. Place all of the ingredients, except the butter, into the pitcher and pulse until the sauce is smooth.

In a small sauce pan, melt the butter over medium-low heat. Add the fig sauce from the blender and bring just to a boil. Reduce the heat to low and simmer, stirring frequently, until the sauce thickens, about 20 minutes. Use at once or cover and store in the refrigerator.

✳TIP

This outrageously wonderful sauce is great when first made when served warm with goat cheese over toasted baguette slices. But, it is even better when stored in the refrigerator for 24 hours and slathered cold over scones or muffins for a special morning treat!

YOU'LL NEED:

✓ 1500ml Pitcher
✓ Blade Assembly
✓ Pitcher Lid

CRANBERRY & ORANGE RELISH

MAKES ABOUT 900ML

This relish is so delish you will want to use it year around! If fresh cranberries are unavailable, use frozen. For variety, add cinnamon, vanilla or a splash of orange liqueur.

1 medium orange, peeled and pulled into quarters
360gm bag fresh cranberries
1 tablespoon sugar, or to taste
1 tablespoon orange liqueur (optional)

Place all ingredients into the pitcher and pulse until finely chopped and uniform. Taste and add more sugar, if desired. Transfer to a storage bowl, cover and chill for at least two hours, allowing the flavours to marry.

✳TIP

You can only imagine how wonderful this relish tastes when combined with chicken or turkey! Try smoothing this relish on whole wheat bread and adding turkey slices, blue cheese crumbles and arugula for an out-of-this-world sandwich.

YOU'LL NEED:

✓ 1500ml Pitcher
✓ Blade Assembly
✓ Pitcher Lid

CHAPTER NINE
Desserts & Sweet Treats

REAL WHIPPED CREAM

SERVES 6

300ml whipping cream
2 tablespoons sugar
1 teaspoon vanilla extract

TIP

For the perfect whipped cream, place the **Master Prep®** Processing Bowl with blades in place, in the refrigerator for 15 minutes before whipping. Cream just whips better when everything is nice and cool.

Place all ingredients in the **Master Prep®** Processing Bowl. Secure the top and pulse in short pulses for 15-25 seconds, or until cream is whipped to the consistency you desire.

Serve immediately. If storing, refrigerate in the **Master Prep®** Processing Bowl with lid on. Whipped cream will deflate over the course of several hours, but stored in the **Master Prep®** Processing Bowl itself, re-whipping will be a snap!

YOU'LL NEED:

✓ 1200ml Bowl
✓ Blade Assembly
✓ Bowl Lid

CHOCOLATE MOUSSE

SERVES 4

300ml whipping cream
3 tablespoons chocolate syrup

TIP

Dish into individual serving bowls and place into the freezer for 2 hours to create a light and fluffy frozen dessert that I would call Instant Ice Cream if making ice cream in the **Ninja® Master Prep®** weren't so easy in its own right!

Place whipping cream and chocolate syrup in the **Master Prep®** Processing Bowl. Secure the top and pulse in short pulses for 15-25 seconds, or until light and fluffy.

Serve immediately. If storing, refrigerate in the **Master Prep®** Processing Bowl with lid on. Mouse will deflate over the course of several hours, but stored in the **Master Prep®** Processing Bowl itself, re-whipping will be a snap!

YOU'LL NEED:

✓ **1200ml Bowl**
✓ **Blade Assembly**
✓ **Bowl Lid**

CHERRY MOUSSE

SERVES 4

12 frozen cherries
300ml whipping cream
2½ tablespoons sugar
¼ teaspoon vanilla extract

✳ TIP

For an amazingly decadent dessert, whip up a batch of all three of my whipped desserts and serve a scoop of each, one on top of the other. Cherry Mousse on the bottom, topped with Chocolate Mousse, topped with Real Whipped Cream.

Place cherries in the **Master Prep®** Chopper. Secure the top and pulse 8-10 times until cherries are well juiced, but somewhat grainy. Set aside cherry mixture until step 3.

Place whipping cream, sugar, and vanilla extract in the **Master Prep®** Processing Bowl. Secure the top and pulse in short bursts for 15-25 seconds, or until fluffy with strong peaks.

Add cherry mixture into whipped cream mixture and pulse 5-7 more short pulses, until well combined. Serve immediately.

YOU'LL NEED:

✓ 500ml Chopper
✓ Blade Assembly
✓ Chopper Lid

WHIPPED CREAM CHEESE FROSTING

SERVES 12

240gms cream cheese
2 tablespoons butter
360gms icing sugar
1 teaspoon vanilla extract
⅛ teaspoon salt

✳ TIP

Substitute 240ml of sour cream in place of the cream cheese for a homemade Sour Cream Frosting that is perfect to top cheesecakes, pastries or even cinnamon rolls!

Place all the ingredients in the **Master Prep®** Processing Bowl. Secure the top and pulse in 5 second bursts, until well combined and fluffy.

Refrigerate for 1-2 hours to firm before frosting your favourite dessert. Keep your frosted, finished desserts refrigerated at all times.

YOU'LL NEED:

✓ 1200ml Bowl
✓ Blade Assembly
✓ Bowl Lid

RULE THE KITCHE

CHOCOLATE FUDGE

SERVES 32

110gms butter
120ml milk
440gms light brown sugar
1 teaspoon vanilla extract
90gms dark chocolate chips
360gms icing sugar

✳ TIP

For a Chocolate Pecan or Walnut Fudge: add in 70gms of pecans or walnuts after step 4, pulsing 3-4 times to roughly chop and combine.

Heat butter in sauté pan over medium high heat until sizzling.

Add milk and brown sugar to pan, stirring constantly. Bring to a boil and cook for 1 minute before removing from heat.

Stir vanilla extract and chocolate into hot brown sugar mixture until fully combined. Let cool for 2-3 minutes until still hot, but not boiling hot.

Place icing sugar in **Master Prep®** Pitcher and cover with chocolate and brown sugar mixture. Secure top and pulse for 10-15 seconds until smooth and fully combined.

Pour finished fudge into an 8x8 baking dish for fudge squares or a small loaf pan for taller, thicker fudge. Refrigerate for at least 3 hours to firm up before slicing into 32 squares.

YOU'LL NEED:

✓ 1500ml Pitcher
✓ Blade Assembly
✓ Pitcher Lid

PEANUT BUTTER FUDGE

SERVES 32

110gms butter
120ml milk
440gms light brown sugar
1 teaspoon vanilla extract
175gms creamy peanut butter
360gms icing sugar

✳ TIP

Peanut butter and chocolate make the perfect match, of course. Make a batch of Peanut Butter Fudge and a batch of my Chocolate Fudge, recipe page: 152 and package 2 squares of each as favors for your next party or get together.

Heat butter in sauté pan over medium high heat until sizzling.

Add milk and brown sugar to pan, stirring constantly. Bring to a boil and cook for 1 minute before removing from heat.

Stir vanilla extract and peanut butter into hot brown sugar mixture until fully combined. Let cool for 2-3 minutes until still hot, but not boiling hot.

Place powdered sugar in **Master Prep**® Pitcher and cover with peanut butter and brown sugar mixture. Secure top and pulse for 10-15 seconds until smooth and fully combined.

Pour finished fudge into an 8x8 baking dish for fudge squares or a small loaf pan for taller, thicker fudge. Refrigerate for at least 3 hours to firm up before slicing into 32 squares.

YOU'LL NEED:

✓ 1500ml Pitcher
✓ Blade Assembly
✓ Pitcher Lid

MARBLED MACADAMIA BARK

SERVES 6

100gms macadamia nuts
190gms semi-sweet chocolate chips
190gms white chocolate chips

✳ TIP

Homemade chocolate bark is probably the easiest, but impressive, gift you can give someone. I like to buy square tins and line them with wax paper, just don't forget the ribbon!

Place macadamia nuts in the **Master Prep**® Chopper. Secure Chopper's top and pulse 3-4 times, until nuts are roughly chopped.

Microwave semi-sweet chocolate chips for about 60-90 seconds, until melted, stopping at least once to stir.

Line a small sheet pan with wax paper, and then pour melted chocolate over top, tilting from side to side to coat the paper.

Microwave white chocolate chips for about 60-90 seconds, until melted, stopping at least once to stir.

Pour white chocolate directly over the semi-sweet chocolate, then use a wooden spatula to swirl and marble together. Sprinkle macadamia nuts over top.

Refrigerate for at least 3 hours to firm up before removing from pan and breaking into smaller pieces to serve.

YOU'LL NEED:

✓ 500ml Chopper
✓ Blade Assembly
✓ Chopper Lid

QUICK AND EASY PIE CRUST

SERVES 8

190gms white flour
3 tablespoons milk
120ml oil
2 teaspoons sugar
1 teaspoon salt

✳ TIP

To bake up the most sturdy pie curst, cover
moulded crust with aluminum foil, pressing
foil down into the crust until it is perfectly
formed to the pan. Fill aluminum foil with
heavy, raw beans before baking to keep
pressure on crust as it bakes.

Preheat oven to 375 degrees Fahrenheit, 190 degrees
Celsius or Gas Mark 5.

Place all ingredients in the **Master Prep**® Processing
Bowl. Secure Processing Bowl's top and pulse for 5
seconds, until all ingredients are well combined.

Press crust mixture evenly into the bottom and walls
of a 9 inch pie pan. Bake for 10 minutes or until lightly
browned

Let cool for 30 minutes before refrigerating until use.

YOU'LL NEED:

✓ 1200ml Bowl
✓ Blade Assembly
✓ Bowl Lid

RULE THE KITCH

CHOCOLATE CHIP POUND CAKE

SERVES 12

550gms yellow cake mix
100gms instant vanilla pudding mix
225gms butter or margarine, softened
4 large eggs
240ml milk
190gms semi-sweet chocolate chips
confectioners sugar, for garnish

✳ TIP

It may not seem like all of the ingredients will fit into the pitcher at first, but I promise you that they will!

Preheat oven to 325 degrees Fahrenheit, 170 degrees Celsius or Gas Mark 3.

Place cake mix, pudding mix, butter, eggs, and milk in the **Master Prep®** Pitcher, secure the top, and pulse in 10 long pulses (about 1 minute all together). Use a rubber spatula and scrape down the walls of the pitcher and then pulse a few more times, until batter is smooth and lump free.

Remove blades and use a rubber spatula to fold the chocolate chips into the batter.

Pour batter into a 12 cup Bundt or tube pan and bake for 60-65 minutes, or until a toothpick inserted into the center comes out mostly clean.

Cool completely before dusting with confectioner's sugar and slicing to serve.

YOU'LL NEED:

✓ 1500ml Pitcher
✓ Blade Assembly
✓ Pitcher Lid

GRAHAM CRACKER PIE CRUST

SERVES 8

75gms graham crackers
3 tablespoons butter or margarine
3 tablespoons sugar

TIP

This works best with slightly softened, but not melted butter. When making a very sweet pie, there's no need to add the additional sugar

Preheat oven to 375 degrees Fahrenheit, 190 degrees Celsius or Gas Mark 5.

Place graham crackers, butter and sugar in the **Master Prep®** Processing Bowl. Secure Processing Bowl's top and pulse for 10 seconds, until cookies are entirely pulverized.

Press cookie mixture evenly into the bottom and walls of a 9 inch pie pan. Bake for 8 minutes

Let cool for 30 minutes before refrigerating until use.

YOU'LL NEED:

✓ 1200ml Bowl
✓ Blade Assembly
✓ Bowl Lid

BANANA CREAM PIE

SERVES 8

1 Quick and Easy Pie Crust, recipe page: 155
240ml non-dairy whipped topping
100gms instant vanilla pudding mix
360ml milk
3 bananas
½ teaspoon banana extract
whipped cream, to top

Prepare, bake and cool one Quick and Easy Pie Crust, according to the directions on that page. Set out non-dairy whipped topping to thaw for about 10 minutes.

Place vanilla pudding mix, milk, 1 peeled banana (reserving the other 2 for step 5), and banana extract in the **Master Prep®** Pitcher. Secure top and pulse for 15-20 seconds, until creamy and lump free.

Pour banana and pudding mixture into a large mixing bowl and gently fold non-diary whipped topping into it with a rubber spatula, just until the two are combined. Do not over mix or the whipped topping will collapse!

Pour the finished pie filling into the Quick and Easy Pie Crust and refrigerate for at least 2 hours, until set.

Peel and slice the remaining 2 bananas into ¼ inch slices. Arrange the slices on top of the set cream filling in an even layer. Garnish with an entire, thick layer of whipped cream and serve immediately.

✳TIP

To keep the fresh, sliced bananas that top this pie from turning brown, you may want to dip them in a small glass of water mixed with 1 tablespoon lemon juice. The trick to cutting the perfect slice is to add the top whipped cream layer after the pie is sliced and on serving plates.

YOU'LL NEED:

✓ 1500ml Pitcher
✓ Blade Assembly
✓ Pitcher Lid

CREAMY KEY LIME PIE

SERVES 8

1 Graham Cracker Pie Crust, recipe page: 157

240gms cream cheese

1 can (420gm) sweetened condensed milk

1 large egg

2 large egg yolks

120ml key lime juice

1 tablespoon sugar

whipped cream, for garnish

TIP

Key lime juice is an absolute must for key lime pie, as it has an entirely different flavour than regular lime juice. You can, however, make a creamy lemon pie by substituting fresh lemon juice and ½ teaspoon of lemon extract.

Preheat oven to 350 degrees Fahrenheit, 180 degrees Celsius or Gas Mark 4 and place pie crust, in pie pan, on a baking sheet.

Place cream cheese, sweetened condensed milk, egg, egg yolks, key lime juice and sugar in the **Master Prep**® Pitcher. Secure top and pulse for 15-20 seconds, until creamy and well combined.

Pour pie filling into crust and shake crust to settle Bake for 12 minutes.

Remove from oven and let cool for 1 hour before refrigerating for at least 2 hours. Serve chilled, topped with whipped cream and a slice of fresh key lime.

YOU'LL NEED:

✓ 1500ml Pitcher

✓ Blade Assembly

✓ Pitcher Lid

WHITE CHOCOLATE RASPBERRY CUPCAKES

SERVES 18

1 box (550gms) white cake mix
1 box (100gms) instant white chocolate pudding mix
320ml water
2 tablespoons butter, melted
1 tablespoon vegetable oil
3 large egg whites
60gms raspberries
80gms icing sugar
1 container white frosting
white chocolate chips

Preheat oven to 350 degrees Fahrenheit, 180 degrees Celsius or Gas Mark 4. Place cake mix, pudding mix, water, butter, vegetable oil, and egg whites in the **Master Prep®** Pitcher, secure the top, and pulse in 10 long pulses (about 1 minute all together). Use a rubber spatula and scrape down the walls of the pitcher and then pulse a few more times, until batter is smooth and lump free.

Use the batter to fill 18-24 cupcakes, lined with paper liners, about 2/3 of the way full.

Bake for 20-25 minutes, or until a toothpick inserted into the center of a cupcake comes out mostly clean. Let cool completely.

Place raspberries and icing sugar in the **Master Prep®** Processing Bowl, secure the top, and pulse in 7 long pulses, until completely blended. Remove blades and use a rubber spatula to gently fold frosting into raspberry mixture. Refrigerate until ready to ice cupcakes.

Use a pastry bag or icing spatula to ice cupcakes with the raspberry frosting. Top each with a few white chocolate chips before serving.

TIP

The raspberry candies (sold in most stores with a large candy section) make a really great garnish for these cupcakes, but fresh raspberries work really well too! You can also use clear edible cake glitter, sold in the baking sections of craft stores.

YOU'LL NEED:

✓ 1500ml Pitcher
✓ Blade Assembly
✓ Pitcher Lid

ALMOND COCONUT MACAROONS

SERVES 12

non-stick cooking spray
95gms almonds
100gms sugar
¼ teaspoon salt
3 large egg whites
1 teaspoon vanilla extract
200gms sweetened coconut flakes

TIP

For stringier, chewier macaroons; do not add coconut in step 3. Add the coconut after the other ingredients are well mixed and use a spoon to combine.

Preheat oven to 325 degrees Fahrenheit, 170 degrees Celsius or Gas Mark 3 and spray a baking sheet with non-stick cooking spray.

Place almonds, sugar and salt in the **Master Prep**® Pitcher. Secure the Pitcher's top and pulse 15-20 seconds until almonds are a well grated, breadcrumb consistency.

Add egg whites, vanilla extract and coconut flakes to the ground almonds and re-secure top. Pulse only 4-5 times until ingredients are well combined, but coconut is still somewhat intact.

Carefully remove blades from Pitcher, and then scoop out mixture, one very rounded teaspoon at a time. Drop onto the greased baking sheet about an inch apart. Bake for 18-20 minutes, until a golden brown. Makes about 24 cookies.

YOU'LL NEED:

✓ 1500ml Pitcher
✓ Blade Assembly
✓ Pitcher Lid

RULE THE KITCHE

CHAPTER TEN
Condiments
& Spice Blends

NATURAL PEANUT BUTTER

SERVES 10

330gms roasted peanuts, unsalted and shelled
60ml vegetable oil
2 tablespoons sugar
½ teaspoon salt

Place all ingredients in the **Master Prep®** Processing Bowl. Secure the top and pulse in 5 second bursts for about 2 minutes, until smooth and creamy.

Store refrigerated. Will keep for about 6 weeks.

YOU'LL NEED:

✓ 1200ml Bowl
✓ Blade Assembly
✓ Bowl Lid

FRESH CUCUMBER RELISH

SERVES 4

1 large cucumber, sliced thick
¼ of 1 small white onion
2 tablespoons cider vinegar
2 teaspoons sugar
½ teaspoon celery salt

Peel cucumber, and then slice in half lengthwise. Spoon out the softer, seed filled portion in the center and discard. Quarter the peeled and cleaned cucumber halves to fit into the **Master Prep**® Processing Bowl.

Place cucumber and all other ingredients in the **Master Prep**® Processing Bowl. Secure the top and pulse in quick bursts for about 15 seconds, until cucumber and onion are diced well. Refrigerate for at least 2 hours before serving to let the flavours mingle.

YOU'LL NEED:

✓ 1200ml Bowl
✓ Blade Assembly
✓ Bowl Lid

AVOCADO MAYONNAISE

SERVES 8

1 avocado, skinned and pitted
1 tablespoon lime juice
1 tablespoon fresh coriander
½ teaspoon salt
60ml olive oil

✳TIP

Set out all of your ingredients before cutting into the avocado to keep it from turning brown before you've had the chance to turn it into mayonnaise. The acidity of the lime juice will stop the process dead in its tracks.

Place avocado, lime juice, coriander and salt in the **Master Prep®** Pitcher. Secure top and pulse for 10 seconds, until combined.

Open pour spout on top of Pitcher and pulse the mixture in 10 second bursts as you slowly drizzle in the olive oil in a thin, yarn-thick stream. Continue this process until all of the olive oil has been combined and mayonnaise is dense and creamy.

Cover and store refrigerated for up to one week.

YOU'LL NEED:

✓ 1500ml Pitcher
✓ Blade Assembly
✓ Pitcher Lid

HOMEMADE MAYONNAISE

SERVES 12

1 large egg
1 large egg yolk
1 tablespoon lemon juice
¼ teaspoon dry mustard
½ teaspoon salt
240ml olive oil

Place egg, egg yolk, lemon juice, dry mustard and salt in the **Master Prep®** Processing Bowl. Secure top and pulse for 10 seconds until combined.

Open pour spout on top of Processing Bowl and pulse the mixture in short bursts as you slowly drizzle in the olive oil in a thin, yarn-thick stream. Continue this process until all of the olive oil has been combined and mayonnaise is dense and creamy.

YOU'LL NEED:

✓ 1200ml Bowl
✓ Blade Assembly
✓ Bowl Lid

RULE THE KITCHE

SMOKED JALAPENO PEPPER MAYONNAISE

SERVES 12

1 batch Homemade Mayonnaise, recipe: 167
1 tablespoon lime juice
1 tablespoon chopped smoked jalapeno pepper
chillies in adobo sauce
1 spring fresh coriander

Prepare the Homemade Mayonnaise recipe as written on page 167, substituting lime juice in place of the lemon juice.

Add smoked jalapeno pepper chillies and fresh coriander to the finished mayonnaise and pulse in 6-8 more short bursts until all is combined.

YOU'LL NEED:

✓ 1200ml Bowl
✓ Blade Assembly
✓ Bowl Lid

SCAMPI BUTTER

SERVES 8

¼ of 1 small red onion
2 cloves garlic, peeled
2 sprigs fresh parsley
1 teaspoon salt
¼ teaspoon ground black pepper
1½ tablespoons lemon juice
¼ teaspoon Worcestershire sauce
110gms unsalted butter or margarine,
slightly softened

Place onion, garlic, parsley, salt, pepper, lemon juice and Worcestershire sauce in the **Master Prep®** Chopper. Secure top and pulse 5-7 times in quick bursts until the garlic and onion begin to break up.

Remove top and use a spoon to push mixture down, away from the walls of the Chopper.

Add butter, re-secure top and pulse in quick bursts for 30-45 seconds, until all ingredients are well combined, but still slightly chunky. Serve immediately or cover and refrigerate.

✳TIP

For the perfect steak topping butter medallions, scoop the finished scampi butter into plastic wrap and then roll it up into a cylinder, twisting both ends. Refrigerate until firm and it's ready to unwrap and slice!

YOU'LL NEED:

✓ 500ml Chopper
✓ Blade Assembly
✓ Chopper Lid

PARMESAN HERB BREADCRUMBS

SERVES 8

1 baguette, sliced thin
1 teaspoon Italian seasoning
60gms Parmesan cheese
1 teaspoon garlic powder
1 teaspoon onion powder
1 teaspoon salt
½ teaspoon sugar
½ teaspoon pepper

✳TIP

A fine, almost powdery consistency will coat chicken and other meats better for sautéing or baking. A coarser, chunky consistency adds more texture to a dish, and is especially good for topping casseroles!

Preheat oven to 425 degrees Fahrenheit, 220 degrees Celsius or Gas Mark 7. Bake bread slices, single layer, on a sheet pan for 8-10 minutes until lightly browned and crunchy.

Place baked bread slices and remaining ingredients in the **Master Prep®** Pitcher. Secure the Pitcher's top and pulse for 10-15 seconds in quick bursts until your desired consistency has been reached.

YOU'LL NEED:

✓ 1500ml Pitcher
✓ Blade Assembly
✓ Pitcher Lid

ASIAN GINGER SPICE BLEND

MAKES ABOUT 75GMS

Fresh ginger contributes a powerful punch of flavour to this fresh mix. Use with chicken or fish for best results.

1-inch piece fresh ginger, peeled
15gms onion powder
20gms garlic salt
15gms black pepper
2 tablespoons red pepper flakes

Place all of the ingredients in the **Master Prep**® Chopper and pulse for 15 seconds, or until the ginger is completely incorporated with the remaining ingredients. Store in a tightly sealed container and refrigerate.

✳TIP

Change up this blend by including lemon pepper, or five spice powder in place of the onion powder. Try adding 60ml of olive oil to create a super fish rub prior to grilling.

YOU'LL NEED:

✓ 500ml Chopper
✓ Blade Assembly
✓ Chopper Lid

RULE THE KITCHE

ITALIAN SEASON MIX

MAKES 50GMS SEASONING

A classic, flavourful blend of savory herbs and spices. Store this herb blend in the refrigerator in a tightly sealed container.

5gms fresh marjoram leaves
1 tablespoon fresh sage leaves
2 tablespoons fresh rosemary
2 tablespoons fresh oregano leaves
2 tablespoons fresh basil leaves
2 tablespoons fresh thyme
2 tablespoons fresh savory (optional)
1 tablespoon black pepper
2 cloves garlic, peeled (or you may use 2 tablespoons garlic salt)

Place all ingredients in the pitcher and pulse until uniform. Use as a rub for beef, or pat on chicken prior to grilling. Store in a tightly sealed container in the refrigerator.

✳TIP

This mix will make enough rub for 2 large steaks or several chicken breasts.

YOU'LL NEED:

✓ 1500ml Pitcher
✓ Blade Assembly
✓ Pitcher Lid

FRESH HOT DOG & HAMBURGER RELISH

MAKES ABOUT 200ML OF RELISH

Take me out to the ballgame with this spicy, sweet and crunchy spread!

1 large white onion, peeled and quartered
1 celery stick
8 sweet pickles or gherkins
1 green bell pepper, cored and seeded, cut in quarters
2 cloves garlic, peeled
60ml canned tomato paste
60ml cider vinegar
1½ tablespoons chilli powder
2 tablespoons dark brown sugar
1 teaspoon Dijon mustard

Place the onion, celery, pickles, pepper and garlic in the pitcher. Pulse until uniformly chopped. The mixture should not be smooth. Add the tomato paste, vinegar, and remaining ingredients. Blend again until uniform. Spoon the relish into a glass or plastic container and cover tightly. Store for up to 2 weeks in the refrigerator.

TIP

Go beyond hamburgers and hot dogs! Pack this relish on top of baked potatoes, toss onto salads, pair up with crackers and cheese, or spread on lunchbox sandwiches in place of mayo or mustard.

YOU'LL NEED:

✓ 1500ml Pitcher
✓ Blade Assembly
✓ Pitcher Lid

RULE THE KITCHE

CREAMY HORSERADISH SPREAD

MAKES 200ML SPREAD

Sharp, piquant horseradish is often overlooked because it can be so over-powering, however it really deserves a spread of its own. Use sparingly with prime rib or any other cut of beef and, as your taste adapts, become a little daring and add more.

3 tablespoons white horseradish (not cream)
120ml sour cream
120ml mayonnaise
pinch salt
pinch black pepper
½ sprig fresh parsley

Place all of the ingredients in the bowl and pulse until smooth. Use a spatula to clean the sides of the pitcher, if needed.

Chill for at least 2 hours before using. Store in a tightly closed container for up to 1 week.

✳TIP

A whole horseradish root doesn't really have much flavour, but cutting into it brings out enzymes that pack a wallop! This spread softens the sharp flavour by combining it with mayonnaise. Substitute sour cream or plain yogurt and add a handful of herbs for a great flavour change.

YOU'LL NEED:

✓ 1200ml Bowl
✓ Blade Assembly
✓ Bowl Lid

MAPLE
CINNAMON
PEACHES & PLUMS
P. 184

CHAPTER ELEVEN
Baby & Toddler Treats

BAKED CRISPY MOZZARELLA STICKS

MAKES 8 CHEESE STICKS

Who can resist crunchy cheese sticks? Boost this already healthy dish by using whole wheat bread and adding wheat germ to the bread crumb mixture.

4 slices stale or day old bread
40gms Parmesan cheese, finely grated
½ teaspoon dried basil
½ teaspoon dried parsley
2 eggs
4 tablespoons milk
8 sticks string cheese
olive or olive oil (can substitute with olive oil)
cooking spray

Place the bread into the pitcher and pulse into medium crumbs. Add the Parmesan cheese, basil and parsley and blend until crumbs are fine. Transfer the bread crumb mixture to a shallow dish. Beat the eggs and milk together in a shallow bowl.

Dip each cheese stick into the egg mixture, coating well, then roll in the bread crumbs. Re-dip in the egg mixture and roll again in the bread crumbs to form a thick crust. Repeat with each cheese stick. Place the cheese sticks on a baking sheet, cover and refrigerate for 30 to 40 minutes.

Preheat the oven to 350°F degrees Fahrenheit, 180 degrees Celsius or Gas Mark 4. Spray cheese sticks with non stick spray or olive oil and bake for 6 to 8 minutes. Watch closely to remove the sticks before the cheese melts. Serve cooled.

YOU'LL NEED:

✓ 1500ml Pitcher
✓ Blade Assembly
✓ Pitcher Lid

HEALTHY MAC & CHEESE

MAKES 8 TO 10 SERVINGS

Pureed carrots add vitamins and colour to a classic kid-favorite!

2 slices stale or day old bread
1 medium carrot, peeled, and steamed
100ml milk
225gms cottage cheese
240gms macaroni, uncooked
150gms cheddar cheese, grated
2 tablespoons unsalted butter

Place the bread in the pitcher and pulse into fine crumbs. Remove the bread crumbs to a small bowl. Place the cooked carrot and milk in the blender and pulse until the carrot is pureed, cleaning the sides of the pitcher with a spatula as needed. Add the cottage cheese and pulse until just blended.

Prepare the elbow macaroni according to the package directions. When the pasta is done, drain in a colander and transfer to 22cm by 33cm baking dish. Add the blended carrot mixture and cheese and stir until the ingredients are well combined.

Preheat the oven to 350°F degrees Fahrenheit, 180 degrees Celsius or Gas Mark 4. Melt the butter in a small saucepan over low heat or in microwave. Toss the bread crumbs with the melted butter and scatter over the top of macaroni. Bake for 30 to 40 minutes, or until top is golden brown and casserole is hot and melty. Cool slightly and serve.

YOU'LL NEED:

✓ 1500ml Pitcher
✓ Blade Assembly
✓ Pitcher Lid

RULE THE KITCHE

BANANA RICE PUDDING

MAKES ABOUT 500ML, ENOUGH FOR 4 TO 6 TODDLER SERVINGS

A tasty and nourishing treat. Rice milk may be substituted for cow's milk if your child has an intolerance to dairy foods.

1 ripe banana, peeled
100gms cooked brown rice
60ml warmed milk (more may be needed)
⅛ teaspoon pure vanilla extract
⅛ teaspoon ground cinnamon

Place all ingredients into the pitcher and pulse until the consistency is appropriate for your child. Use a spatula to clean the sides of the blender as necessary. If the pudding is too thick, add additional milk. Serve right away or cover and store in refrigerator.

TIP

Even little ones appreciate the great spice flavours of vanilla and cinnamon. Serve warmed with a little bit of butter for a special treat.

YOU'LL NEED:

✓ 1500ml Pitcher
✓ Blade Assembly
✓ Pitcher Lid

SMOOTH BAKED APPLE

MAKES ABOUT 225GMS, ENOUGH FOR 2 TO 3 TODDLER SERVINGS

Sweeter apples work best for this dish, as apples such as Granny Smith may be too tart for your baby.

1 medium apple, cored
½ teaspoon pure maple syrup
1 whole cinnamon stick (or ½ teaspoon ground cinnamon)
1 tablespoon ricotta cheese

Preheat the oven to 350 degrees Fahrenheit, 180 degrees Celsius or Gas Mark 4. Place the apple on a large piece of foil. Drizzle maple syrup over the top and into the core of apple. Place the cinnamon stick into core. Loosely wrap foil up around apple, twisting at the top to seal and place on a baking dish. Bake for 35 to 40 minutes, until the apple is very soft.

Remove the apple from the oven, discard the cinnamon stick and while still warm, but cool enough to handle, peel the apple if desired. Place into the pitcher and pulse until the apple is almost pureed. Add the ricotta cheese to the apple and pulse to combine. Serve warm or cover and store in refrigerator until use.

YOU'LL NEED:

✓ **1500ml Pitcher**
✓ **Blade Assembly**
✓ **Pitcher Lid**

PARSNIPS, POTATO AND PEARS, OH MY

MAKES ABOUT 500ML, ENOUGH FOR 6 TO 8 TODDLER MEALS

The pears add a lovely sweetness to this nutrient packed trio.

1 medium garnet yam or sweet potato, peeled, halved lengthwise and thickly sliced
1 medium parsnip peeled, halved lengthwise and thickly sliced
1 small pear, peeled, cored and chopped
pinch ground nutmeg
pinch ground cinnamon

In a medium saucepan, place the yam and parsnip in about 500ml of water and bring to a boil over medium-high heat. Reduce the heat, cover and simmer until the vegetables are almost softened. Add the pear and continue cooking until tender, about 6 minutes.

Drain, reserving the cooking water and transfer the cooked fruit and vegetables into the pitcher, along with the nutmeg and cinnamon. Pulse until the mixture is pureed and smooth. Add some of the reserved cooking water if a thinner consistency is desired. Serve warm or cover and store in refrigerator.

YOU'LL NEED:

✓ 1500ml Pitcher
✓ Blade Assembly
✓ Pitcher Lid

PERFECTLY PEACHY CHICKEN

MAKES 500ML TO 700ML, ENOUGH FOR 8 TO 10 BABY/TODDLER SERVINGS

This complete healthy meal is a sweet way to get protein into your little ones.

1 small boneless, skinless chicken breast, cut into 1 inch pieces
1 small sweet potato or garnet yam, peeled, and cut into 1 inch pieces
240ml to 360ml apple juice
½ fresh peach, peeled, pitted and chopped

Place the chicken and potato in a small saucepan and add enough apple juice to cover. Bring just to a boil over medium-high heat, reduce to medium-low and simmer until almost tender. Add the peach and continue cooking until tender, about 4 to 6 minutes.

Drain off any remaining apple juice and reserve. Place the cooked chicken, potato and peach into the pitcher and pulse until pureed, adding some of the reserved apple juice to obtain your desired consistency. Use immediately or cover and store in the refrigerator, reheating before serving.

YOU'LL NEED:

✓ 1500ml Pitcher
✓ Blade Assembly
✓ Pitcher Lid

RULE THE KITCHE

MAPLE CINNAMON PEACHES & PLUMS

MAKES ABOUT 500ML, ENOUGH FOR 6 TO 8 BABY/TODDLER SERVINGS

This yummy healthy dessert is sweet without the addition of sugar.

1 large ripe peach, peeled, halved and pitted
2 fresh ripe plums, quartered
240ml plain yogurt
1 teaspoon pure maple syrup
pinch ground cinnamon

Place the peach and plums into the bowl and pulse until pureed. Add the yogurt, maple syrup and cinnamon, mixing to blend. Serve or cover and store in the refrigerator. Makes about 500ml, enough for 6 to 8 baby/toddler servings.

✳TIP

Puree the peach and plums in your **Ninja®** *blender* until very smooth and use this peachy plum dessert within a few days while fresh. This recipe does not freeze well, but can be stored in the refrigerator for up to 2 days.

YOU'LL NEED:

✓ **1200ml Bowl**
✓ **Blade Assembly**
✓ **Blade Lid**

CHEESE & AVOCADO QUESADILLAS

MAKES 2 TO 4 SERVINGS TODDLER SERVINGS

Mixing the butternut puree with the cheese is a great way to get your toddlers to eat their vegetables.

1 small butternut squash, halved and seeded
75gms canned pinto beans, drained
1 avocado, peeled, pitted and chopped
50gms cheddar cheese, grated
4 whole wheat tortillas
olive oil cooking spray

Preheat the oven to 400 degrees Fahrenheit, 200 degrees Celsius or Gas Mark 6. Place the butternut squash on a baking sheet, flesh side down and bake for 45 to 50 minutes. When cool enough to handle, scoop out the flesh and transfer to the pitcher. Pulse until the squash is pureed, about 2 minutes. Measure about 100ml of the puree for the recipe and store the remaining puree, covered, in the refrigerator for another use. Clean the blender and dry.

Spray the underside of 2 tortillas with olive oil cooking spray and place on a baking sheet. Place the beans and avocado in the pitcher and pulse until smooth. Spread the mixture over the 2 tortillas. Combine the butternut squash puree with the cheddar cheese and crumble over the beans.

Place the 2 remaining tortillas on top and spray with the olive oil. Bake for 5 or 6 minutes, or until the cheese melts and the outside of the tortillas are crisp. Serve with a mild salsa, if desired.

YOU'LL NEED:

✓ 1500ml Pitcher
✓ Blade Assembly
✓ Pitcher Lid

GREEN BEANS WITH ROASTED RED BELL PEPPER DIP

MAKES 2 TO 4 SERVINGS

The roasted red pepper puree makes a sweet nutritious dip and the green beans are easy for little hands to grip!

1 large red bell pepper, washed
20 fresh green beans, washed and strings removed

Using tongs, hold the red bell pepper over the flame of a gas burner or place under the broiler in the oven. Turn frequently to blacken on all sides. Place the pepper into a paper bag and let sit for 10 to 12 minutes. Remove the pepper from bag and easily slip off the outer skin. Cut the pepper in half and remove the seeds.

Place the roasted, seeded pepper into the pitcher and pulse until pureed and very smooth.

Steam the green beans until just tender. Cool and serve to your toddler with roasted red bell pepper puree for dipping.

YOU'LL NEED:

√ **1500ml Pitcher**
√ **Blade Assembly**
√ **Pitcher Lid**

GOLDEN MASHED POTATO PUFFS

MAKES ABOUT 24 PUFFS

Cheesy, warm and wonderful, these puffs will get the attention of kids and adults alike!

4 medium russet potatoes, peeled and diced
120ml milk, warmed
1 egg, beaten
½ teaspoon baking powder
2 teaspoons white flour
40gms Parmesan cheese, grated
½ teaspoon salt

In a large saucepan filled with water, bring the potatoes to a boil, and then reduce the heat to medium-low and simmer until tender. Drain the potatoes and place into the pitcher. Add the remaining ingredients, reserving 2 tablespoons of Parmesan cheese, and pulse until blended.

Preheat the oven to 350 degrees Fahrenheit, 180 degrees Celsius or Gas Mark 4. Drop the potato mixture by teaspoons onto a non-stick baking sheet. Sprinkle the potato puffs with the remaining Parmesan cheese and bake for 20 minutes. Allow the puffs to cool slightly and serve warm.

YOU'LL NEED:

✓ 1500ml Pitcher
✓ Blade Assembly
✓ Pitcher Lid

RULE THE KITCHEN

INDEX

A

ALMONDS

Almond Coconut Macaroons, 161

Almond Crusted Chicken, 110

Cranberry Almond Muffins, 95

AMERICAN CHEESE

Mexican Cheese Dip, 59

APPLES

Apple Carrot Blast, 26

Apple, Cranberry & Gorgonzola Salad, 131

Green Apple Goodness Smoothie, 19

Healthy Fruit and Vegetable Smoothie, 15

Homemade Apple Sauce, 80

Smooth Baked Apple, 181

Veggie Iron Power Punch, 10

APRICOTS

Asian Ginger Spice Blend, 171

ARTICHOKE

Microwave Spinach and Artichoke Dip, 57

ASPARAGUS

Cream Of Asparagus Soup, 78

AVOCADOS

Avocado Mayonnaise, 166

Cheese & Avocado Quesadillas, 185

Chicken Tortilla Soup, 86

Thick and Chunky Guacamole, 58

B

BACON

Chopped Salad, 126

Quiche Lorraine Cups, 68

BALSAMIC VINEGAR

Fresh Fig Sauce, 144

Balsamic Grilling Sauce, 143

BANANAS

Banana Cream Pie, 158

Banana Rice Pudding, 180

South Pacific Slush, 52

Strawberry Banana Smoothie, 13

BASIL

Basil Pesto, Fresh, 82

BEANS

Cheese & Avocado Quesadillas, 185

Classic Hummus, 61

Cuban Black Bean Soup, 79

Green Beans with Roasted Red Pepper
Dip, 186

Really Veggie Burgers, 129

Refried Kidney Beans, 117

Tuscan White Bean Dip, 60

BEEF

Blue Cheese Sliders, 70

Cracker Crumb Meatloaf, 112

Ground Sirloin Stuffed Peppers, 113

Italian Style Meatballs, 105

Steak and Cheese Burgers, 127

Swedish Meatballs, 114

BEER

Cowboy Mopping Sauce, 142

Bellini, Italian, 50

BELL PEPPERS

Chicken Tortilla Soup, 86

Cool and Creamy Gazpacho, 74

Fresh Hot Dog & Hamburger Relish, 173

Green Beans with Roasted Red Pepper
Dip, 186

Ground Sirloin Stuffed Peppers, 113

Roasted Butternut Squash Soup, 75

Roasted Pepper Cheese Dip, 62

BEVERAGES

Apple Carrot Blast, 26

Breakfast Veggie Blend, 8

Bushwacker, 51

Mudslide, 44

Chocolate Raspberry Rumble, 35

Cranberry Twist, 29

Creamy Pina Colada, 41

Fresh Watermelon Slush, 24

Frozen Blue Bayou, 46

Frozen Cuban Mojito, 49

Frozen Lemonade, 27

Garden in a Glass, 9

Italian Bellini, 50

Key Lime Pie Ice, 34

The Best Frozen Margarita, 40

Mocha Cappuccino, 25

Mudslide, 44

Orange and Cream, 33

Orange Russian Tea, 12

Peach Daiquiri, 43

Pineapple Breeze, 28

Pineapple Mango Mojito, 48

Sea Breeze Soother, 53

South Pacific Slush, 52

Strawberry Daiquiri, 42

Triple Berry Twist, 11

Tropical Paradise Blend, 16

Vanilla Coffee Ice, 32

Veggie Iron Power Punch, 10

"White" Mango Ice, 30

Bisque, Classic Lobster, 91

BISCUITS

Almond Coconut Macaroons, 161

Homestyle Biscuits, 94

BLACKBERRIES

Triple Berry Twist, 11

BLUEBERRIES

Berry Mixed Up Smoothie, 14

Boldly Blueberry Muffins, 96

BLUE CHEESE

Apple, Cranberry & Gorgonzola Salad, 131

Blue Cheese Sliders, 70

Blue Cheese Spread, 70

BLUE CURACAO

Frozen Blue Bayou, 46

BRANDY

Fresh Fig Sauce, 144

BREAD

Breakfast Veggie Blend, 8

BROCCOLI

Broccoli and Cheese Soup, 77

Chopped Salad, 126

BROWNIES

Awesome Brownies, 101

BRUSCHETTA

Roasted Tomato & Olive Bruschetta, 71

BURGERS

Blue Cheese Sliders, 70

Fresh Hot Dog & Hamburger Relish, 173

Really Veggie Burgers, 129

Salmon Burgers, 128

Steak and Cheese Burgers, 127

Turkey Burgers, 130

Bushwacker, 51

BUTTER

Natural Peanut Butter, 164

Peanut Butter Cookies, 99

Peanut Butter Fudge, 153

Scampi Butter, 169

BUTTERNUT SQUASH

Roasted Butternut Squash Soup, 75

Cheese & Avocado Quesadillas, 185

C

CAKES

Awesome Brownies, 101

Carrot Cake, 100

Chocolate Chip Pound Cake, 156

White Chocolate Raspberry Cup Cakes, 160

CARROTS

Apple Carrot Blast, 26

Breakfast Veggie Blend, 8

Carrot Cake, 100

Healthy Fruit and Vegetable Smoothie, 15

Mandarin Orange Smoothie, 18

CARROT JUICE

Mandarin Orange Smoothie, 18

CAULIFLOWER

Roasted Garlic Smashed Cauliflower, 116

CHEDDAR CHEESE

Broccoli and Cheese Soup, 77

Cheese & Avocado Quesadillas, 185

Chopped Salad, 126

Roasted Pepper Cheese Dip, 62

Steak and Cheese Burgers, 127

CHEESE. *See individual cheeses*

CHERRIES

Cherry Mousse, 150

CHICKEN

Almond Crusted Chicken, 110

Chicken Tortilla Soup, 86

Perfectly Peachy Chicken, 183

Your Choice Chicken Salad, 125

CHILLIES

Chicken Tortilla Soup, 86

Chimichurri Sauce, South American, 89

Cool and Creamy Gazpacho, 74

Smoked Jalapeno Pepper Mayonnaise, 168

Smoking Smoked Jalapeno Pepper Sauce, 135

CHOCOLATE

Chocolate Chip Pound Cake, 156

Chocolate Fudge, 152

Chocolate Mousse, 149

Chocolate Raspberry Rumble, 35

Cookies and Cream Milkshake, 36

Marbled Macadamia Bark, 154

Protein Packed Mocha Smoothie, 17

White Chocolate Raspberry Cupcakes, 160

COCONUT

Almond Coconut Macaroons, 161

Creamy Pina Colada, 41

Strawberry Mango Colada, 45

COCONUT MILK

Pineapple Breeze, 28

South Pacific Slush, 52

COCONUT LIQUEUR

Bushwacker, 51

COFFEE

Mocha Cappuccino, 25

Protein Packed Mocha Smoothie, 17

Vanilla Coffee Ice, 32

COFFEE LIQUEUR

Mudslide, 44

COINTREAU. *See Orange flavoured liqueur*

COOKIES AND BARS

Baked Meringue Cookies, 98

Cookies and Cream Milkshake, 36

Peanut Butter Cookies, 99

Cowboy Mopping Sauce, 142

CORN

Really Creamed Corn, 118

Southern Cornbread Muffins, 119

CRANBERRIES

Cranberry Almond Muffins, 95

Apple, Cranberry & Gorgonzola Salad, 131

Cranberry & Orange Relish, 145

Cranrazz Smoothie, 21

Cranberry Twist, 29

Sea Breeze Soother, 53

Cream Real Whipped, 148

CRANBERRY JUICE

Cranberry Juice, 53

CREAM CHEESE

Apple, Cranberry & Gorgonzola Salad, 131

Herbed Cheese Dip, 56

Mexican Cheese Dip, 59

Roasted Pepper Cheese Dip, 62

Quiche Lorraine Cups, 68

Whipped Cream Cheese Frosting, 151

CRÈME DE CACAO

Bushwacker, 51

CUCUMBERS

Apple, Cranberry & Gorgonzola Salad, 131

Cool and Creamy Gazpacho, 74

Fresh Cucumber Relish, 165

Greek Cucumber Sauce, 81

D

Daiquiri, Strawberry, 42

Daiquiri, Peach 43

DESSERTS

Banana Cream Pie, 158

Banana Rice Pudding, 180

Creamy Key Lime Pie, 159

Ninja® Snow Cones, 31

DIPS

Classic Hummus, 61

Green Beans with Roasted Red Pepper
    Dip, 186

Herbed Cheese Dip, 56

Mexican Cheese Dip, 59

Microwave Spinach and Artichoke Dip, 57

Roasted Pepper Cheese Dip, 62

Thick and Chunky Guacamole, 58

Tuscan White Bean Dip, 60

E

ESPRESSO. *See Coffee*

EGGS

Baked Meringue Cookies, 98

Easy Hollandaise Sauce, 85

Extra Creamy Egg Salad, 123

Homemade Mayonnaise, 167

Light and Fluffy Deviled Eggs, 69

Quiche Lorraine Cups, 68

Smoked Jalapeno Pepper Mayonnaise, 168

F

Fig Sauce, Fresh, 144

FRUITS. *See also individual fruits*

Healthy Fruit and Vegetable Smoothie, 15

G

Garden in a Glass, 9

GARLIC

Cool and Creamy Gazpacho, 74

Roasted Garlic Smashed Cauliflower, 116

South American Chimichurri Sauce, 89

Yukon Gold Mashed Potatoes, 120

GINGER

Asian Ginger Spice Blend, 171

Healthy Fruit and Vegetable Smoothie, 15

Graham Cracker Pie Crust, 157

GRAND MARNIER

See Orange flavoured liqueur

GRAPE JUICE

Cranberry Twist, 29

"White" Mango Ice, 30

GRAPEFRUIT JUICE

Sea Breeze Soother, 53

Greek Herb Rub, 140

Greek Cucumber Sauce, 81

GUACAMOLE

Thick and Chunky Guacamole, 58

H

HAM

Ham Salad, 124

Herbed Cheese Dip, 56

Horseradish Spread, Creamy, 174

Hot Dog & Hamburger Relish, Fresh, 173

I

IRISH CREME LIQUEUR

Mudslide, 44

Italian Bellini, 50

Italian Seasoning Mix, 172

Italian Style Meatballs, 105

K

KAHLUA
Bushwacker, 51

Kansas City BBQ Sauce, 138
Key Lime Pie, Creamy, 159

KIWI
Tropical Paradise Blend, 16

L

Lasagne Style Penne Bake, 106

LEMONADE
Frozen Lemonade, 27
Frozen Blue Bayou, 46

LEMONS
Apple Carrot Blast, 26
Frozen Blue Bayou, 46
Frozen Lemonade, 27
Lemon & Herb Marinade, 136

LIMES
Cranberry Twist, 29
Creamy Key Lime Pie, 159
Fresh Tomato Salsa, 64
Fresh Watermelon Slush, 24

Frozen Cuban Mojito, 49
Peach Daiquiri, 43
Key Lime Pie Ice, 34
Orange Papaya Shrimp Marinade, 137
Smoked Jalapeno Pepper Mayonnaise, 168
Smoking Smoked Jalapeno Pepper Sauce, 135
Strawberry Daiquiri, 42
Sweet and Spicy Pineapple Salsa, 66

LIME JUICE
Strawberry Daiquiri, 42

Lobster Bisque, Classic, 91

M

Mac & Cheese, Healthy, 179

MACADAMIAS
Marbled Macadamia Bark, 154

MANGOES
Pineapple Mango Mojito, 48
Strawberry Mango Colada, 45
Tropical Paradise Blend, 16
"White" Mango Ice, 30

Maple Cinnamon Peaches & Plums, 184

MANGO JUICE
"White" Mango Ice, 30

MARGARITAS
The Best Frozen Margarita, 40

MARINADES
Lemon & Herb Marinade, 136
Orange Papaya Shrimp Marinade, 137
Smoking Smoked Jalapeno Pepper Sauce, 135
Teriyaki Grilling Marinade, 134

MINT
Frozen Cuban Mojito, 49

MOJITO
Frozen Cuban Mojito, 49
Pineapple Mango Mojito, 48

Mopping Sauce, Cowboy, 142

MOZZARELLA CHEESE
Baked Crispy Mozzarella Sticks, 178

Mudslide, 44

MUFFINS
Boldly Blueberry Muffins, 96
Cranberry Almond Muffins, 95
Southern Cornbread Muffins, 119

MUSHROOMS
Marvellous Stuffed Mushrooms, 67
Really Veggie Burgers, 129

N

Ninja® Pizza, 109
Ninja® Snow Cones, 31

O

OLIVES

Chunky Olive Spread, 63
Olive Tapenade Bruschetta, 71

ONIONS

Fresh Hot Dog & Hamburger Relish, 173

ORANGE DRINK

Fresh Fig Sauce, 144
Mandarin Orange Smoothie, 18
Orange and Cream, 33
Orange Russian Tea, 12
South Pacific Slush, 52

ORANGE FLAVOURED LIQUEUR

Strawberry Daiquiri, 42

ORANGES

Cranberry & Orange Relish, 145
Fresh Fig Sauce, 144
Mandarin Orange Smoothie , 18
Orange Papaya Shrimp Marinade, 137
Orange Russian Tea, 12
Smoking Smoked Jalapeno Pepper Sauce,
     135
South Pacific Slush, 52

P

PAPAYAS

Orange Papaya Shrimp Marinade, 137

Paprika Rub, Sweet, 141

PARMESAN CHEESE

Fresh Basil Pesto, 82
Golden Mashed Potato Puffs, 187
Herbed Cheese Dip, 56
Italian Style Meatballs, 105
Lasagne Style Penne Bake, 106
Parmesan Herb Breadcrumbs, 170
Turkey Meatloaf With Sun-Dried
     Tomatoes and Parmesan, 108

PARSLEY

Greek Herb Rub, 140
South American Chimichurri Sauce, 89

Parsnips, Potato and Pears, Oh My, 182

PASTA

Healthy Mac & Cheese, 179
Lasagne Style Penne Bake, 106
No-Cook Pizza and Pasta Sauce, 84

PEACHES

Honey Sweet Peach Smoothie, 20
Italian Bellini, 50
Maple Cinnamon Peaches & Plums, 184
Peaches and Cream Milkshake, 37
Peach Daiquiri, 43

Perfectly Peachy Chicken, 185

PEANUTS

Natural Peanut Butter, 164
Peanut Butter Cookies, 99
Peanut Butter Fudge, 153
Peanut Dipping Sauce, 90

PEARS

Parsnips, Potato and Pears, Oh My, 182

Pesto, Basil, 82

PECANS

Pecan Crusted Salmon, 111

PICKLES

Fresh Hot Dog & Hamburger Relish, 173

PIES

Banana Cream Pie, 158
Creamy Key Lime Pie, 159
Graham Cracker Pie Crust, 157
Quick and Easy Pie Crust, 155

PINEAPPLE

Creamy Pina Colada, 41
Pineapple Breeze, 28
Pineapple Mango Mojito, 48
Sweet and Spicy Pineapple Salsa, 66

PINEAPPLE JUICE

Healthy Fruit and Vegetable Smoothie, 15
Tropical Paradise Blend, 16

PISTACHIO

Pistachio Crusted Tilapia, 104

PIZZA

Homemade Pizza Sauce, 88
No-Cook Pizza and Pasta Sauce, 84
Ninja® Pizza, 109

Plums & Peaches, Maple Cinnamon, 184

PORK. *See also Bacon; Ham*

Spinach Stuffed Pork Loin, 107

POTATOES

Golden Mashed Potato Puffs, 187
Parsnips, Potato and Pears, Oh My, 182
Potato Pancakes, 122
Twice Baked Sweet Potatoes, 121
Yukon Gold Mashed Potatoes, 120

PROSCIUTTO. *See Ham*

Pudding, Banana Rice, 180

Q

Quesadillas, Cheese & Avocado, 185
Quiche Lorraine Cups, 68

R

RASPBERRIES

Berry Mixed Up Smoothie, 14
Chocolate Raspberry Rumble, 35
Cranrazz Smoothie, 21
Raspberry Coulis, 83
Triple Berry Twist, 11
White Chocolate Raspberry Cup Cakes, 160

RELISHES

Cranberry & Orange Relish, 145
Fresh Cucumber Relish, 165
Fresh Hot Dog & Hamburger Relish, 173

Rice Pudding, Banana, 180

RICOTTA

Lasagne Style Penne Bake, 106
Spinach Stuffed Pork Loin, 107

RUBS

Greek Herb Rub, 140
Sweet Paprika Rub, 141

RUM

Bushwacker, 51
Creamy Pina Colada, 41
Frozen Cuban Mojito, 49
Peach Daiquiri, 43
Pineapple Mango Mojito, 48
Strawberry Mango Colada, 45
South Pacific Slush, 52
Strawberry Daiquiri, 42

S

SALAD DRESSINGS

Lemon & Herb Marinade, 136

SALADS

Apple, Cranberry & Gorgonzola Salad, 131
Chopped Salad, 126
Extra Creamy Egg Salad, 123
Ham Salad, 124
Your Choice Chicken Salad, 125

SALMON

Pecan Crusted Salmon, 111
Salmon Burgers, 128

SALSAS. *See Sauces and salsas*

SAUCES AND SALSAS

Avocado Mayonnaise, 166
Balsamic Grilling Sauce, 143
Cowboy Mopping Sauce, 142
Confetti Coleslaw, 115
Easy Hollandaise Sauce, 85
Fresh Basil Pesto, 82
Fresh Fig Sauce, 144
Fresh Hot Dog & Hamburger Relish, 173
Fresh Tomato Salsa, 64
Greek Cucumber Sauce, 81
Homemade Apple Sauce, 80
Homemade Mayonnaise, 167
Homemade Pizza Sauce, 88
Kansas City BBQ Sauce, 138

Peanut Dipping Sauce, 90

Raspberry Coulis, 83

No-Cook Pizza and Pasta Sauce, 84

Smoked Jalapeno Pepper Mayonnaise, 168

Smoking Smoked Jalapeno Pepper Sauce, 135

South American Chimichurri Sauce, 89

Sweet and Spicy Pineapple Salsa, 66

Sea Breeze Soother, 53

Scampi Butter, 169

SHAKES

Cookies and Cream Milkshake, 36

Peaches and Cream Milkshake, 37

SHRIMP

Orange Papaya Shrimp Marinade, 137

Sliders, Blue Cheese, 70

SMOOTHIES

Berry Mixed Up Smoothie, 14

Cranrazz Smoothie, 21

Green Apple Goodness Smoothie, 19

Healthy Fruit and Vegetable Smoothie, 15

Honey Sweet Peach Smoothie, 20

Mandarin Orange Smoothie, 18

Protein Packed Mocha Smoothie, 17

Strawberry Banana Smoothie, 13

Triple Berry Twist, 11

SOUPS

Broccoli and Cheese Soup, 77

Chicken Tortilla Soup, 86

Classic Lobster Bisque, 91

Cool and Creamy Gazpacho, 74

Cream Of Asparagus Soup, 78

Cream of Tomato Soup, 76

Cuban Black Bean Soup, 79

Roasted Butternut Squash Soup, 75

South American Chimichurri Sauce, 89

South Pacific Slush, 52

SOUR CREAM

Mexican Cheese Dip, 59

Thick and Chunky Guacamole, 58

Yukon Gold Mashed Potatoes, 120

SPICE BLENDS

Asian Ginger Spice Blend, 171

Italian Seasoning Mix, 172

SPINACH

Breakfast Veggie Blend, 8

Really Veggie Burgers, 129

Spinach Stuffed Pork Loin, 107

Veggie Iron Power Punch, 10

Microwave Spinach and Artichoke Dip, 57

SPREADS

Blue Cheese Spread, 70

Chunky Olive Spread, 63

Creamy Horseradish Spread, 174

STRAWBERRIES

Berry Mixed Up Smoothie, 14

Healthy Fruit and Vegetable Smoothie, 15

Strawberry Banana Smoothie, 13

Strawberry Daiquiri, 42

Strawberry Mango Colada, 45

Triple Berry Twist, 11

SWEET POTATOES & YAMS

Parsnips, Potato and Pears, Oh My, 182

Perfectly Peachy Chicken, 183

Swedish Meatballs, 114

SWISS CHEESE

Quiche Lorraine Cups, 68

T

TEA

Orange Russian Tea, 12

Veggie Iron Power Punch, 10

TEQUILA

Teriyaki Grilling Marinade, 134

The Best Frozen Margarita, 40

TILAPIA

Pistachio Crusted Tilapia, 104

TOMATOES

Chicken Tortilla Soup, 86

Cool and Creamy Gazpacho, 74

Cream of Tomato Soup, 76

Cuban Black Bean Soup, 79

Fresh Hot Dog & Hamburger Relish, 173

Fresh Tomato Salsa, 64

Garden in a Glass, 9

Healthy Fruit and Vegetable Smoothie, 15

Homemade Pizza Sauce, 88

Kansas City BBQ Sauce, 138

Roasted Tomato & Olive Bruschetta, 71

Turkey Meatloaf With Sun-Dried
Tomatoes and Parmesan, 108

TORTILLAS

Cheese & Avocado Quesadillas, 185

Chicken Tortilla Soup, 86

TURKEY

Turkey Burgers, 130

Turkey Meatloaf With Sun-Dried
Tomatoes and Parmesan, 108

TRIPLE SEC. *See Orange flavoured liqueur*

V

VANILLA

Cookies and Cream Milkshake, 36

Cranrazz Smoothie, 21

Key Lime Pie Ice, 34

Orange and Cream, 33

Peaches and Cream Milkshake, 37

Vanilla Coffee Ice, 32

VEGETABLES. *See also individual vegetables*

Breakfast Veggie Blend, 8

Really Veggie Burgers, 129

Veggie Iron Power Punch, 10

VODKA

Frozen Blue Bayou, 46

Mudslide, 44

Sea Breeze Soother, 53

W

WALNUTS

Apple, Cranberry & Gorgonzola Salad, 131

Your Choice Chicken Salad, 125

WATERMELONS

Fresh Watermelon Slush, 24

WINE

Fresh Fig Sauce, 144

Italian Bellini, 50

Y

YAMS. *See Sweet potatoes and yams*

YOGHURT

Cranrazz Smoothie, 21

Honey Sweet Peach Smoothie, 20

Orange and Cream, 33

Mandarin Orange Smoothie , 18

Protein Packed Mocha Smoothie, 17